REPURPOSING COMPOSITION

REPURPOSING COMPOSITION

Feminist Interventions for a Neoliberal Age

SHARI J. STENBERG

UTAH STATE UNIVERSITY PRESS
Logan

© 2015 by the University Press of Colorado

Published by Utah State University Press
An imprint of University Press of Colorado
5589 Arapahoe Avenue, Suite 206C
Boulder, Colorado 80303

 The University Press of Colorado is a proud member of
The Association of American University Presses.

The University Press of Colorado is a cooperative publishing enterprise sup-
ported, in part, by Adams State University, Colorado State University, Fort
Lewis College, Metropolitan State University of Denver, Regis University,
University of Colorado, University of Northern Colorado, Utah State
University, and Western State Colorado University.

∞ The paper used in this publication meets the minimum requirements of the
American National Standard for Information Sciences—Permanence of Paper
for Printed Library Materials. ANSI Z39.48-1992

ISBN: 978-0-87421-991-3 (paperback)
ISBN: 978-1-60732-388-4 (ebook)

Cover photo courtesy Conant Metal & Light (www.conantmetalandlight.com).

Parts of chapter 2 were included in "Teaching and (Re)Learning the Rhetoric
of Emotion," in *Pedagogy* 11(2): 349–369. © 2011 Duke University Press. All
rights reserved. Reprinted by permission.

Publication supported, in part, by an Enhance grant from the University of
Nebraska's College of Arts and Sciences.

Library of Congress Cataloging-in-Publication Data

Stenberg, Shari J.
  Repurposing composition : feminist interventions for a neoliberal age /
Shari J. Stenberg.
     pages cm
  Includes bibliographical references and index.
    ISBN 978-0-87421-991-3 (pbk.) — ISBN 978-1-60732-388-4 (ebook)
  1. English language—Rhetoric—Study and teaching. 2. Feminism and educa-
tion. I. Title.
  PE1404.S795 2015
  808'.04207—dc23
                      2014044812

24 23 22 21 20 19 18 17 16 15   10 9 8 7 6 5 4 3 2 1

For Jason, Zoe, and Anika

CONTENTS

ACKNOWLEDGMENTS

Through the long process of writing and revising this book, I am deeply grateful to my family, friends, and colleagues, who have supported, inspired, and challenged me. Chris Gallagher has served as a second set of eyes on my drafts for well over a decade, offering incisive, insightful response that never fails to encourage and forward my ideas. Debbie Minter not only read and responded to my drafts with care and support but also administered the writing program while I was on leave to work on this project. Perhaps most important, Debbie's friendship and colleagueship bring joy to my daily work, as she helps me see (and focus on) what is possible.

Teaching the course Rhetoric of Women Writers, which Joy Ritchie developed and then generously handed over to me my first semester at the University of Nebraska–Lincoln, first inspired this project. I am grateful for the path Joy carved for so many women, and for her enduring support. The composition faculty at UNL—Rachel Azima, Robert Brooke, Amy Goodburn, June Griffin, Debbie Minter, and Stacey Waite—provide inspiration, insight and a spirit of collaboration that sustains me. I thank them for their support, directly and indirectly, of this project. I am also thankful to Zach Beare, Marcus Meade, Lauren Gatti, James Crews and Katie Hupp, for reading drafts or talking through ideas. Thanks also to my Nebraska Writing Project Humanities Institute writing group, Sally Hunt and Jen Stastney, whose interest and encouragement helped me over a formidable revision hurdle. The writing advice of my mentor and friend Steve North often plays in my head and keeps me afloat: you've gotta show up, and if it's not working, just take it apart and start again. I appreciate the wisdom of the students whose writing appears in the book; their work inspires and instructs.

Matt Wilson and John Munson provide the soundtrack to my life; I'm forever grateful.

I am indebted to Michael Spooner for his gentle guidance, and for seeing value in what he called my "sober optimism" about change in higher education. I am thankful to Robin DuBlanc for her careful copyediting and to Laura Furney for her help with the production process. I thank Dan Pratt for his care in designing a cover that beautifully illuminates the ideas in the book.

Finally, I thank my husband, Jason, and daughters, Zoe and Anika, who light the way.

The writing of this book was supported by a faculty development leave and an ENHANCE grant from the University of Nebraska–Lincoln.

REPURPOSING COMPOSITION

INTRODUCTION

Jessica Mindich designs sleek, delicately hammered bangle bracelets. Each bracelet is embossed with its own number and the word Newark: the serial number of the illegal gun from which it was made and the city where it was seized. Mindich created her jewelry line, the Caliber Collection, after hearing Newark, New Jersey, mayor speak on the devastating effects of gun violence to the city. With the mayor's support, Mindich began a program to salvage the brass and steel remains of illegal pistols, shotguns, and shell casings confiscated by Newark police and to repurpose the scraps as jewelry. She returns 20 percent of her proceeds to the Newark Police Department's gun buyback program.

The bracelets are meant to be more than a fashion statement, or even a vehicle for fund-raising. Mindich designed the bangle to ensure that its structure reflects its source. The bracelet is oval, not round, to mirror the trigger cage of a gun. It arrives in an evidence bag—no ribbons or bows—imprinted with the story of the jewelry's origins, and the belief that repurposing weapons to raise both awareness and funds improves the caliber (double meaning intended) of the community. In an interview in Time *magazine, Mindich quotes one of her customers, who aptly summarizes her project's purpose: "Caliber bracelets are real guns, real lives saved, literally leading to future guns coming off the streets. You have repurposed guns. The power of guns [has] always been associated with the hand of a shooter. Now people can use guns to make peace" (Nelson 2013).*

*

The Wellington Craftivism Collective is an online feminist community that melds crafting with community building and activism. The collective is part of the larger movement of craftivism, which emerged early in the twenty-first century as a response to consumerism, environmental destruction, and the general sense of hopelessness that surfaced after the 9/11 attacks (Greer 2007). As the name suggests, the movement

DOI: 10.7330/9781607323884.c000

promotes a symbiotic relationship between crafting and activism, repurposing activities often relegated to the domestic sphere—knitting, quilting, baking—to public, activist ends.

The Wellington group hosts regular "Stitch N Bitch" sessions, where members talk politics, teach stitching, and work on projects like patches for their internationally traveling "Occupy" quilt. The collective sponsors workshops on sustainable construction, bike repair, and local food. And it organizes "Street Outreach," delivering baked goods to local shelters.

As Betsy Greer describes it, the movement aims both to engage creativity to serve political ends and to "bring back the personal into our daily lives to replace some of the mass produced" (Greer 2007, 401).

*

In Nancy Judd's (2011) TEDx talk, she wears a dress fashioned from yellow plastic caution tape, recovered from the side of a road. Titled "Caution Dress," it is one of many garments in Judd's line, Recycled Runway, a collection of dresses that repurpose plastic bags, rusty nails, and broken glass to stunning ends. The gowns, however, are not just aesthetically compelling; they are educationally engaging—designed, as Judd says in her TED talk, to "help people see trash with new eyes." Her aim is both to encourage conservation and to challenge consumerism. Fashion, she reasons, is a good way to broach the dialogue. "Most people respond well to a pretty dress," she explains. "I really enjoy these ironies— a pretty dress that's made out of trash that is commenting on the very system that it appears to belong to."

In order to reach a wide audience, Judd's exhibitions are displayed in shopping malls and airports as well as museums. But her art is not limited to its products; she also makes dressmaking a communal, educational process, inviting her audiences—from schoolchildren to adults— to participate by writing a pledge about how they will "live lighter on the earth": each pledge is later sewn to a dress. Her purpose is to help her audiences see trash differently: not as waste, but as wasted resources.

*

These projects are but three examples of feminist repurposing, a practice of locating and enacting imaginative possibilities for change and agency within—and often out of—prohibitive, and even damaging, cultural conditions. These examples are contemporary incarnations of a long line of feminist resistance and resilience, where women find ways—overtly and covertly—to locate *kairos* within existing circumstances and to create their own available means of persuasion. Indeed, a look at women's writing and social contributions across history shows that repurposing is an ancient practice.

In the fourteenth and early fifteenth century, for instance, Julian of Norwich repurposed scripture, then deployed to limit women's roles to procreation and child rearing, to rearticulate God as feminine and to name Jesus as "our true mother" (Julian of Norwich 2001, 27). In the seventeenth century, Sor Juana Inés de la Cruz entered the convent to attain an intellectual life. There, she composed plays and poetry and advocated for women's access to education. During the U.S. Civil War, women used quilts to communicate subversive political messages understood only by fellow quilters (Benson, Olson, and Rindfleisch 1987). And some scholars argue that African American slave women used quilts to encode maps to navigate the Underground Railroad (Sambol-Tosco 2004).

While the term *repurposing* certainly overlaps with and encompasses similar practices like revising, reclaiming, and reappropriating, I feature "repurposing" because of its relevance in both contemporary culture and the field of rhetoric and composition. In a time of economic strain, a Google search of "repurposing" yields a bounty of blogs written by women who describe ways to repurpose domestic and salvage items to new, and often innovative and beautiful, ends. This is not only a means to save money in a tight economy, it is also an ecologically sound practice designed to make use of what is available for new purposes. It is a practice that further involves illuminating, and working within and against, the conditions that characterize a given situation.

In composition and rhetoric classrooms, we want our students to explore and determine their own purposes for writing. We know that effective writing is tied to students' investment in their own projects, in purposes that are student determined, not solely teacher determined. The field has also sought to establish its own disciplinary and curricular purposes, challeng-ing conceptions of itself as a feminized service provider. As I highlight in chapter 1, feminist scholars have played a key role in repurposing seemingly "neutral" practices and approaches to the rhetorical tradition, the composing process, and peda-gogy so as to create more expansive understandings of writing and opportunities for writers. Now, as we face increased neolib-eral pressures to streamline and standardize education—from prepackaged distance learning curricula to machine-scored writing—it is a crucial time for the field to argue for the value of purposes we determine based on our local work with students, our dialogue with one another, and our research.

And so just as the artists' projects described above illuminate the problematic conditions to which they respond—cultures of violence, consumption, and isolation—this book aims to illumi-nate, and argue for repurposing, the problems and practices of neoliberal influences on postsecondary education.

NEOLIBERALISM AND THE UNIVERSITY

While the term *neoliberalism* may not yet readily populate our vocabularies, like most dominant ideologies, its influence is so prevalent as to be rendered invisible, or to seem inevitable—just "the way things are." Indeed, neoliberal values are at work when students choose courses and place them in virtual "shopping carts" or quantify their instructors' "easiness" and appearance on ratemyprofessors.com; when faculty must compete for exter-nal funds to support their regular work; and when private play-ers like the Bill and Melinda Gates Foundation and the Koch brothers, with their deep pockets and political sway, shape the direction of higher education.

Neoliberalism is a set of economic principles and cultural politics that positions the free market as a guide for all human action, substituting for, as Paul Treanor argues, "all previously existing ethical beliefs." "Liberal" here references economic, not political, ideology; it seeks to remove all barriers to the free market, upholding an ideal in which entrepreneurs and private enterprise—not the state or federal government—control the economy (Treanor 2005). Neoliberalism, then, also prizes individualism and individual responsibility. Individuals are regarded as rational economic actors who are expected to make choices that will maximize their human capital. To be rational, according to neoliberal logic, is to act in service of profit (Brulé 2004; Saunders 2010). There is no distinction between the economy and society; what's best for one is considered best for the other.

Since neoliberalism privileges private interests, it encourages the privatization of public services and institutions (Welch 2005). The university is no exception. Since the late 1970s, when state and federal contributions to higher education were severely cut, universities have become ever more reliant on private funding sources (Readings 1996; Saunders 2010; Slaughter and Rhoades 2004). As a result, we see expanded university-corporate partnerships; outsourcing of dining halls, bookstores, and health centers to private vendors; and demand for applied research that commercializes its products.

Even more dramatically, private foundations are increasingly moving in to reform education, often without the input of educators or public debate. At the K–12 level, the Bill and Melinda Gates Foundation both bankrolled the Common Core State Standards movement, to the tune of $200 million, and built the political support necessary to convince state governments to make expensive changes to education (Layton 2014). Gates, along with the Lumina Foundation and billionaire brothers Charles and David Koch, are also making deep inroads in postsecondary education. Since 2006, for instance, the Gates Foundation has spent $472 million on a neoliberal brand of education reform that favors "a system of education designed for maximum measurability, delivered increasingly through technology, and—[as] critics say—narrowly focused on equipping students for short-term employability" (Perry, Field, and Supiano 2013).

This is most evident in the push for competency-based education, a model gaining support from both the federal government and private foundations, which remakes education into a low-cost, individually paced track without credit hours, seat time, or faculty. Students demonstrate their progress by showing mastery of 120 "competencies," such as "can use logic, reasoning, and analysis to address a business problem" (Perry, Field, Supiano 2013). In place of in-class time with tenure-line faculty and peers, adjunct instructors act as individual "coaches," guiding students to resources and assessing their progress. The result is what Debra Humphreys, vice president for policy and public engagement of the Association of American Colleges and Universities, describes as a "hyped-up get it done fast mentality" (Mangan 2013). This mentality applies not only to the time it takes to earn a degree but also to education reform, as it removes dialogue among educators and communities and restricts public conversations about the purpose and process of education.[1]

A heightened pressure for efficiency also shapes how universities are administered. Top-down business models replace shared governance that incorporates faculty and student input into education decisions (Saunders 2010, 58). This shift is not only financial but also ideological, such that "revenue generation, efficiency, and competition" have come to define the priorities of higher education and, in turn, to alter the roles and practices of students and faculty members (56).

With higher tuition bills and student fees, combined with shifts in financial aid from grants to loans, students have come to be the "chief financers" of their own education—a designation that translates their role into that of consumers of education. In efforts to attract students, institutions "advertise education as a service and a life style" (Slaughter and Rhoades 2004, 1), bombarding them with marketing materials—touting luxury dorms and espresso bars—as early as their sophomore year in high school. Parents, too, are encouraged to view college as a commodity, one whose features they can compare in periodicals like *Maclean's* and *U.S. News and World Report*, just as they might when purchasing a car or laptop computer.

Students are not simply costumers in the academic marketplace, however. They are also considered both the "inputs" and "outputs" of their education (Slaughter and Rhoades 2004,

43). As Slaughter and Rhoades summarize, "Student identities are flexible, defined and redefined by institutional market behaviors." For instance, universities seek students who are high scorers on standardized tests, because advertising these numbers increases the presumed prestige of the institution, and, in turn, makes recruitment of future students easier. Once enrolled, students are "captive markets" for the products provided by the universities' corporate partners, found in union stores and restaurants, vending machines and at sporting event concession stands (2). Upon graduation, students become the products, or outputs, of their institutions, with student success—especially in terms of earnings—signaling institutional excellence (44). And then, of course, they become potential donors to the institutions.

Faculty roles are also altered. As universities mimic corporate structures, faculty labor is "unbundled," with the bulk of undergraduate teaching assigned to part-time instructors, teaching assistants, and postdoctoral positions. This both lowers instructional costs and creates a flexible workforce, the members of which do not, typically, have a say in the governance of the university or, often, the curriculum they teach. Tenure-line faculty within a neoliberal climate are expected to compete and produce, with more emphasis placed on generating revenue and less on institutional decision making (Saunders 2010, 54). Patricia Harkin describes how this climate impacts compositionists, as we must increasingly compete for funds to "do the work that has been historically entrusted to us, work that used to be sustained by university and department operating budgets, work that, when grant applications are unsuccessful, no longer gets done" (Harkin 2006, 30–31). She draws from Althusser's notion of interpellation, or being hailed, to argue that in the contemporary university, we are called as "funded researchers"—or, we might say, academic entrepreneurs (32). As a result, she argues, we are prompted to do work that is fundable rather than work that emerges out of problems or interests we encounter as teachers and administrators (33). We are guided, like good neoliberal subjects, by economics.

Neoliberal values also encroach upon writing instruction. In a view of education as job training, writing becomes a masterable, commodified skill whose purpose is deployment in the workplace. Other purposes for writing—civic engagement, personal inquiry, exploration of unfamiliar perspectives—become ancillary to more "profitable" ends. And since neoliberal logics value a streamlined approach to predetermined outcomes or competencies, there is little tolerance for learning processes that entail engagement of (an often recursive) process, collaboration and dialogue among learners, and reflection—in other words, exactly the kind of learning research in composition and rhetoric promotes.

Indeed, neoliberal logic carves education into a narrow path, with a singular purpose: to prepare the future workforce and bolster the economy. While preparing students to find meaningful work and to earn a living is certainly a valid goal of education, I argue that it is not enough. We must also prepare students as civic participants and community members, as writers and thinkers who are able to listen to and engage tension and difference, and as agents in the local contexts that matter to them. This means repurposing education as a complex, relational practice, one that involves, as I argue in chapter 5, learning to respond well to others.

In response to this upsurge of neoliberal pressure, my project turns to feminist thought for two reasons. First, the neoliberal emphasis on rationalism, standardization, and efficiency places feminist values and practices at risk of containment, making it crucial to illuminate them. Second, contemporary and historical feminist scholarship in rhetoric, composition, and pedagogy offers some of the most visible and effectual repurposing efforts in our field, yielding rich examples of re-visioning and reenacting our classrooms, institutions, and intellectual traditions—and in so doing, makes room for new approaches to writing, knowing, collaborating, and assessing. Such efforts offer us both knowledge and practices needed to repurpose our work as writing teachers, sponsors of teacher development, and writing program administrators in the face of neoliberal pressure.

REPURPOSING THE UNIVERSITY

Even as contemporary universities are deeply entangled in neoliberal logic, there still exists possibility for change and movement. In fact, the central premise of this book is that university education, and the practices that comprise it, can be repurposed. Following Slaughter and Rhoades, I argue that an academic capitalist regime has not simply *replaced* a public-good regime; rather, "the two coexist, intersect, and overlap" (Slaughter and Rhoades 2004, 29). After all, even as universities are enmeshed in pressures of accountability, competition, and corporate accommodation, they also tout, and seek to enact, commitments to diversity, creativity, and outreach. While the two purposes of education are often at odds, their coexistence means that there is potential to reclaim and illuminate the public-good approach. This potential is realized only through our local actions. Indeed, academic subjects (professors, students, administrators, and so on) *enact* neoliberal values through specific practices. Or as Slaughter and Rhoades put it, the university is composed of actors who initiate academic capitalism; we are not merely "players being 'corporatized'" (12). This means that by changing our practices, we can alter the purposes and values of our pedagogical sites.

Neoliberal ideology, however, tends to hide in the open, making it difficult at times to see. And so, the first step of repurposing neoliberal practices is to illuminate their very presence. Feminist scholarship is helpful in this regard, due to its long history of highlighting and challenging notions held to be natural and neutral, and instead pointing to how these constructs are ideologically, socially constructed, and—as contemporary scholars argue—*enacted* through specific practices (Jung 2005; Kopelson 2006; LeCourt and Napoleone 2011). For instance, Judith Butler famously frames gender as an identity "instituted through a stylized repetition of acts" that are so commonly repeated as to seem natural (Butler 1988, 519). When gender is understood as something that is enacted and repeated, possibilities emerge for "a different sort of repeating" that breaks or subverts the repetition (520). As a result, gender may be (re)made anew. The first step of feminist repurposing, then, involves highlighting and critiquing existing conditions. We see this work in the examples above, wherein the Caliber bracelets illuminate the problem of gun violence and Judd's dresses highlight the problems of consumerism and waste. In the pages ahead, I show how illuminating normative neoliberal assumptions allows us to break familiar repetitions, working toward purposes and practices in keeping with feminist values.

Feminist repurposing also involves inquiring into and analyzing social context to consider where possibilities exist for working both within and against current structures, systems, and practices. Judd's dresses, made from consumer waste, offer a vivid example of this practice, as she taps into public interest in fashion and consumption in order to challenge the systems that spur these cultural habits. The Wellington Craftivism Collective repurposes the domestic sphere, once considered a "natural" feminine—and thus devalued—domain, into a site of feminist activism. These projects invoke familiar systems and repurpose them, and in so doing, they ask us to view dominant perspectives differently.

Another practice of feminist repurposing is to reclaim what has been cast off or suppressed to be used for new ends. We see this literally in Mindich's repurposing of gun remains or Judd's reuse of plastic caution tape, and repurposing metaphorical "excess" is also a trope in feminist rhetoric and pedagogy. In her 1975 theory of *écriture féminine*, second-wave feminist Hélène Cixous contends that within traditional rhetoric, "the orator is asked to unwind a thin thread, dry and taut." (Cixous 2001, 285). Women, on the other hand, "like uneasiness, questioning. There is waste in what we say. We need that waste" (285). Referring simultaneously to the female voice and the female body, which she sees as intimately connected, Cixous embraces what is typically deemed "excess"—words, digressions, flesh, emotion.

In their article "Excessive Moments and Educational Discourses That Try to Contain Them" Mimi Orner, Elizabeth Ellsworth, and Janet Miller call attention to "excess" pedagogical moments that highlight the relationship between educational discourses and repression (Orner, Miller, and Ellsworth 1996). By considering the excess, they underscore what has been occluded, tamped down, or ignored in dominant educational conversations. The excess—which evokes multiple readings—allows us to see the normative differently, and to locate new possibilities within that which is typically deemed "waste." As Judd contends, waste may be a wasted resource.

Finally, feminist repurposing locates and enacts new possibilities for teaching and learning, for relating to one another, and for enacting cultural change. It creates something new out of existing conditions. The above examples show these possibilities, which include beautiful dresses, quilts, and bracelets, but also extend beyond these products to include opportunity for conversation, sharpened awareness, and seeds for further change.

In the pages ahead, I show how these tactics may be used to repurpose our classroom pedagogies, to work with new teachers, and to enact assessment. Illuminating the act of repurposing is important to my project, since neoliberalism often presents itself as the only viable option. For instance, in her study of new faculty members' construction of professional identities in neoliberal contexts, Louise Archer finds that at the same time the faculty she interviews are critical of the managerial, product-oriented contexts they work within, they simultaneously begin to view neoliberal culture as the only "thinkable" context (Archer 2008, 272). As a result of neoliberalism's pervasiveness, it becomes difficult for these new faculty members to establish a common language of critique that highlights what is lost and to imagine possibilities for an "otherwise" (282). My hope is that my book helps contribute in both ways—to elucidate and critique neoliberal culture and to render visible possibilities for repurposing. Archer reminds us that important moments of resistance often occur at the microlevel, and as I illuminate practices of repurposing in classroom moments, student writing, and assessment work, my hope is to spur readers to consider how resistance and repurposing do or can occur in their own contexts, so that a new repetition might be created—one that disrupts the entrenched mode of neoliberalism.

LOOKING AHEAD

Chapter 1 traces the specific methods through which feminist scholars in rhetoric, composition, and pedagogy have repurposed conceptions of the rhetorical tradition, composition pedagogy, and writing subjects. As I examine their tactics, I build the definition of feminist repurposing that carries throughout the project.

Chapter 2 explores the neoliberal privileging of rationalism by examining dominant cultural tropes for understanding emotion which, in turn, shape educational settings. In particular, I feature the "emotional intelligence" movement as one example of mainstream response to emotion that influences both corporate and pedagogical sites. Alternatively, I challenge approaches that rely on rationalism to discipline—and make efficient—emotion. Building upon the growing body of feminist scholarship that argues for emotion as epistemological (Boler 1999; Micciche 2007; Quandahl 2003; and Worsham 1998), I argue for a pedagogy that repurposes emotion as a crucial part of rhetorical education. I insist we must not stop at analyzing pathos as a rhetorical appeal, but also repurpose emotion as a source of knowledge production—to value what is deemed "excessive" as a resource. To argue for this pedagogy, I show how we can use public texts—in this case, media responses to emotion portrayed by Barack Obama and Hillary Clinton—to illuminate and challenge naturalized conceptions of emotion. I then move on to the text of my classroom to offer examples of engaging emotion as intellectual, rhetorical work.

Chapter 3 examines how neoliberal values shape listening as it relates to argument and dialogue in our culture and, subsequently, in our classrooms. I begin by investigating a trend in corporate culture to value listening—and listening training—which is marketed as a deployable skill that can promote individual agendas and, ultimately, corporate gains. This is a model embraced not only in business but also in educational settings; in fact, I contend that it shapes our teaching of argument, where others' perspectives are used rather than engaged. Here, listening is derived from a divided notion of *logos* that privileges speech above listening, with listening as a means to sharpen one's ability to persuade (Fiumara 1995; Ratcliffe 1999). In contrast, feminist scholarship repurposes listening to strive toward a restored logos, where listening and speech/writing function in productive interplay. Drawing from classroom moments and student writing, I show how rhetorical listening (Ratcliffe 1999) can alter the way teachers and learners conceive of and practice our engagement with others, how we understand our own positions, and how we compose arguments.

I then move to examine conceptions of teacher agency and belonging in a neoliberal climate that removes teachers' bodies, knowledge, and commitments from the scene of education. Chapter 4 elucidates neoliberal discourse as constitutive and gendered; it teaches us whom to be and how to belong in (and to) academic settings, where self-commodification and acclimation serve as the pathway to agency. For marginalized subjects, then, to attain neoliberal agency often requires the denial of embodied locations, knowledge, and history. In contrast, feminist scholars have long argued that the margins offer a revealing lens through which to view dominant culture (Collins 1986; hooks 1990), such that embodied knowledge is a channel both to clarify epistemological possibilities and to take responsibility for the partiality of one's perspective. These arguments offer a revised mode of *enacting* agency that insists upon illuminating traits covered by neoliberalism: embodiment, location, and responsibility to and connection with one another.

In the final chapter, I rely on the feminist ethic I've established throughout the book to argue for repurposing responsibility as a commitment to students, teachers, the field, and our communities. Here I examine how responsibility is typically framed within an accountability logic that is heavily influenced by neoliberal values. Accountability claims a "view from everywhere" but does not often include the views of teachers and learners or consider local contexts (Fleckenstein 2008). In contrast, I call for repurposing educational responsibility as necessarily relational, context sensitive, and evocative of the question "How can we respond well?" (Adler-Kassner and Harrington 2010; Thiem 2008).

This notion of responsibility forwards the feminist values, knowledges, and practices I articulate in the preceding chapters: situated, reflexive knowledge; careful listening and genuine dialogue; and acknowledgment of learning as complex and affective. In so doing, I offer examples of institutions, programs, and individuals that demonstrate a responsibility approach to teaching and learning as an alternative to a top-down accountability logic.

One of the most powerful consequences of neoliberal ideology and tactics is its tendency to exclude alternatives and rival forms of thought (Saunders 2010, 49). Feminist perspectives, on the other hand, aim to expand our collective view, to support more inclusive knowledge practices and purposes, and to insist that teaching and learning are relational, embodied, and affective processes. In the pages ahead, I aim to offer practices and perspectives that provide alternatives to neoliberal logic and that help illuminate possibilities for our daily local work with students, new teachers, and one another.

NOTE

1.   For a fuller discussion of the consequences of competency-based education and its relationship to composition and rhetoric, see Gallagher (2016), "Our Trojan Horse: How Compositionists Were Duped into Promoting Competency-Based Education (and Our Own Irrelevance) through Outcomes Assessment and What We Can Do about It Now."

1

FEMINIST REPURPOSING IN RHETORIC, COMPOSITION, AND PEDAGOGY

In her 1973 essay, "Toward a Woman-Centered University," Adrienne Rich calls attention to the masculinist arrangement of university curricula, pedagogy, and purposes—and to the cloak of neutrality it wears. "When a woman is admitted to higher education," she writes, "it is often made to sound as if she enters a sexually neutral world of 'disinterested' and 'universal' perspectives" when, in fact, "the structure of relationships, [and] even the style of discourse, including assumptions about theory and practice, ends and means, process and goal" are decidedly male centric (Rich 1979, 134, 136). In response, Rich challenges her feminist readers to work at once within and against the existing institutional structure in order to imagine and enact possibilities beyond it. To do so is to re-create a university that benefits not only women but all who work within it, by making room for multiple ways of knowing and being (134). We might see Rich's work, then, as a call for repurposing the institution, for locating possibilities, complexities, and contradictions within it, and then for finding ways to remake it into something else, a something else that is more spacious, expansive, and reflexive for all of its inhabitants.

While our institutions today have by no means achieved Rich's ideal, we can point to many ways in which her vision now animates our daily landscape. Women and gender studies programs flourish; curricula feature contributors representing diverse racial, ethnic, and sexual identities; diversity and difference are embraced in many university mission statements. In rhetoric and composition, the body of feminist scholarship on rhetoric, composition, and pedagogy

DOI: 10.7330/9781607323884.c001

continues to grow, examining the politics of gender in sites ranging from local classrooms to the rhetorical tradition to international relations.

And yet, the cloak of neutrality Rich observed in 1973 has not disappeared from our institutions—it has, perhaps, merely changed designs, now obscuring (and sometimes not even bothering to hide) a decidedly neoliberal agenda. Within neoliberal logic, there is no distinction between the economy and society; what's best for one is considered best for the other. Neoliberalism views the free market as a benevolent force, distrusts state intervention and regulation of the economy, and regards the individual as a rational economic actor (Saunders 2010, 45). Here, education becomes an economic enterprise in service of the market, with students as rational consumers who make choices based on economics, and faculty as managed or managerial professionals.

In our contemporary climate, workforce production is assumed to be the primary purpose of education, feeding the larger aim of bolstering the nation's position in the global market. As Cochran-Smith and Lytle observe, "In much of the discourse about public education, it is now considered self-evident that the nation's place in the global economy depends on the quality of its educational system" (Cochran-Smith and Lytle 2009, 8). Because a discourse of "self-evidence" informs the tie between the university and the market, a corporate approach is conflated with common sense. Consequently, the values of the neoliberal university tend to be cloaked in the discourse of inevitability—it's just the way it is—and neutrality—"It's not about politics, it's about money" (Weber 2010, 128). Here, of course, an economic exigency is so naturalized as to seem neutral.

In this book I contend that now is a vital time to illuminate the values and practices that compose the neoliberal institution and then to look for ways we might enact it differently. As Judith Butler observes of gender, we need to first understand what appears normal or neutral—who we read as a woman, say, or a queer woman—as informed by a "stylized repetition of acts" (Butler 1988, 519). Once we see how norms are constituted by a repetition of enactments, we can locate possibilities for disrupting the pattern so as to create new possibilities for a "different sort of repeating" (520). It is this new repetition that I focus on here, articulated as repurposing.

In what follows, I mine our field's history to uncover moments of feminist repurposing in the areas of rhetoric, composition, and pedagogy. Here, my aim is to illuminate key examples of feminist enactments that broke the repetition of presumed neutrality and normalcy in order to create new alternatives for all speakers and writers. I define repurposing as a practice that involves (1) attending to and challenging the habitual or status quo, (2) drawing on and departing from these existing conditions, and (3) moving to articulate and enact new purposes.

Indeed, a look back at rhetoric and composition's history reveals many moments of repurposing elements of our field, including writing, first-year writing programs, and the role of writing students and teachers. I focus in particular on feminist scholars' repurposing efforts for two reasons. First, in a neoliberal culture centered on "rational" individuals and knowledge practices, feminist perspectives need to be made clear so that they are not contained or lost by pressures to narrowly define educational practices and purposes. Second, contemporary and historical feminist scholarship in rhetoric, composition, and pedagogy offers some of the most compelling repurposing efforts in our field, providing instructive examples of re-visioning and reenacting our pedagogies and scholarly practices. As feminist scholars including Patricia Hill Collins (1986), bell hooks (1990), and Donna Haraway (1988) have well established, there is much to be learned from the keen views produced on the margins. In the pages ahead, I excavate tactics[1] of feminist repurposing from the landscape of rhetoric and composition to show how this work is embedded in our field's history. These tactics, I argue, become resources to draw upon during a moment when our field's values are often in tension with neoliberal purposes.

FEMINIST REPURPOSING OF RHETORIC

I begin with the work of feminist rhetorical studies because it offers one of our field's clearest examples of teachers and scholars appropriating a tradition that is at once ripe with potential and steeped in masculine ancestry. The work in feminist rhetorical studies, which surfaced in the 1980s and gained momentum in the 1990s, is centered on the prefix *re*: recover, reclaim, rescue, restore, retheorize, revise. While technically "re" indicates a repetition, within feminist rhetorical work, the prefix functions as a disruption that draws on what exists *and* opens a pathway for a new set of practices. That is to say, it repurposes rhetoric. Indeed, as the presence of feminist rhetorical studies has grown, we see recurrences of work that moves beyond adding to or critiquing the current tradition; increasingly, these texts and studies do both at once, appropriating and revising the classical tradition to alter the very conception of rhetoric.

Kathleen Ryan (2006) provides one rendering of feminist rhetorical studies' evolution in "Recasting Recovery and Gender Critique as Inventive Arts: Constructing Edited Collections in Feminist Rhetorical Studies." She traces two distinct epistemic and methodological threads in the field's early literature—recovery and gender critique—with the former focused on the addition and inclusion of women's voices in the rhetorical canon and the latter on revising and retheorizing the tradition. Ryan marks three linear phases of edited collections, beginning with a strict divide between recovery and critique (with texts like Karlyn Kohrs Campbell's 1989 *Man Cannot Speak for Her* and Shirley Wilson Logan's 1995 *With Pen and Voice: A Critical Anthology of Nineteenth-Century African-American Women* on the recovery side and the 1992 special issue of *Rhetoric Society Quarterly*, "Performing Feminisms, Histories, Rhetorics," edited by Susan Jarratt [1992], representing gender critique). The next stage of edited collections, she argues, is built upon a causal relationship between recovery and gender critique, such that the addition of women's voices to the tradition results in new approaches to theorizing and enacting rhetoric (for instance, she notes that the introduction to Lunsford's 1995 *Reclaiming*

Rhetorica focuses on chronological recovery while the ending—
the outcome—prompts readers toward gender critique). Ryan
concludes with an analysis of Joy Ritchie and Kate Ronald's 2001
Available Means and a special issue of *Rhetoric Society Quarterly*,
"Feminist Historiography in Rhetoric" (Bizzell 2002a), which
she categorizes as enacting a both/and approach in which
recovery and gender critique occur simultaneously. Here, as
Ryan observes, "gender critique opens up possibilities for recovery because this art entails challenges to gendered assumptions
about the contexts and content of rhetoric previously taken as
foundational and recovered texts become rhetorical theory and
sites for criticism and theorizing" (Ryan 2006, 36). This both/
and approach, she contends, is most promising for the field's
future scholarship and, I would add, a necessary component of
repurposing rhetorical study and practice.

While I agree with Ryan that scholarship in feminist rhetorical studies moves progressively toward a both/and approach,
my reading suggests that rather than three distinct movements,
we can observe a growing recurrence of what I label feminist
repurposing.[2] Thanks to those who have recovered and recast
women's speech and writing as rhetoric, there is evidence of
women rhetors from across history working within and against
conventions and norms to create new purposes with and for
their words. And as Jacqueline Jones Royster and Gesa Kirsch
argue in their book *Feminist Rhetorical Practices*, now that a large
body of feminist rhetorical scholarship exists, we can observe
repetitions of strategies and methodologies that "have broken
through habitual expectations" of a tradition historically "about
men and male-dominated arenas." (Royster and Kirsch 2012,
17). These disruptions create "volatility in research and practice, tectonic shifts on the rhetorical landscape," which they
see as ripe with potential to facilitate continued transformation
of the field (17). Following a similar path, my aim is to locate
feminist disruptions and revisions of the habitual within rhetorical studies that illuminate possibilities for *repurposing* not only
rhetoric and composition but also the institutional contexts
and practices in which we engage the discipline. I turn now to

highlight some of the key practices and patterns—which create a new kind of repetition—employed by feminist scholars to repurpose rhetoric.

RECOVERY AS REPURPOSING

As I've suggested above, feminist repurposing requires viewing the normative or habitual as context specific and value laden. While the omission of women in the rhetorical canon is perhaps glaring to contemporary eyes, the deep-seated values and assumptions inherited from that masculinist tradition tend to remain so naturalized as to appear universal. As Cheryl Glenn observes, rhetoric as we have known it is "*exclusively* upper-class, male, agonistic, and public—yet seemingly universal" (1997, 2). Feminist scholars shed light on the contradiction borne by a tradition at once upheld as "universal"—a sphere into which anyone, presumably, can enter, with equal potential to speak and to be heard—and at the same time decidedly male centric and exclusive.

Challenging the neutrality of the rhetorical tradition has aided historical recovery work, helping us to better understand the cultural conditions that rendered women's presence invisible. We learn, for instance, that the near absence of women in classical rhetoric transpired from the fact that women in fifth-century Athens were utterly silenced; in fact, because women were denied citizenship, the language did not even have a word for a woman from Athens (Loraux 1993, 10). Women were deprived of education, literacy, citizenship, and even entry to the public sphere, except during religious festivals. In the words of Aristotle, "Between the sexes, the male is by nature superior and the female inferior, the male ruler and the female subject" (Aristotle 1944, 1.254b). By contextualizing ancient Greece through a gendered lens, feminist scholars make clear the exigency for recovering a greater range of perspectives and underscore the limited scope of a rhetorical tradition designed to train the male elite for public oratory. But feminist scholars also seek possibilities and ruptures in a tradition that at first glance appears monolithic; it is by "listening—and listening hard" (Lunsford 1995, 6) and recognizing silence as a "fertile field of investigation" (Glenn 1997) that they discover traces of women's contributions.

Cheryl Glenn's recovery of Aspasia, a rhetorician, philosopher, political influence, and teacher of male rhetoricians in fifth-century Athens—whose influence and speech is rendered only through the words of men—offers a rich example of mining silence for voice. Because Glenn articulates her process, uncertainties, and development of a methodology, her work also illuminates the process of repurposing.

Breaking a habitual pattern often requires not only studying and critiquing it but making the difficult decision to move away from what is valued—or in this case, to move toward that which has been culturally ostracized. Glenn explains that before she could recover Aspasia, she had to release the grip of the "paternal narrative" that cast Aspasia as either "apocryphal or a glorified prostitute" and unverifiable, due to her appearance only in secondary sources (Glenn 1997, 5). To reclaim someone deemed an illegal immigrant as a citizen of history, Glenn has to approach the process of historical inquiry differently.

She begins by illuminating the normative as constructed, showing that the accepted narrative of Aspasia resulted from particular lenses, particular modes of engaging history, neither of which served her purposes as a feminist historiographer. In contrast, she embraces a performative feminist historiography which, she writes, embodies a "promise of connecting women and history and rhetoric" and points to a "simultaneously committed and utopian rhetorical world, in which women's participation is not always upstaged, dubbed over, or completely ignored by men" (Glenn 1997, 11). This approach allows her to step out of normative, fixed notions of history (How can I write Aspasia into history as it is predominantly understood? How can I add her into the given narrative?) to *name her own purpose* for rhetorical historicizing.

To construct a rhetorical world in which women's participation is recognized requires both drawing from existing historical records and conventions and engaging in critical imagination (Royster and Kirsch 2012) to depart from them. To cast Aspasia in a new historical role, Glenn considers how others have written into history those who exist only as traces or whispers, or who have been billed as outcasts. She turns to the collection of work on the Sophists, examining how historiographers practiced "the crafts of resurrection, animation, and even ventriloquism to re-present them" (Glenn 1997, 8). In addition, she considers Socrates, whose words, like Aspasia's, do not exist in any primary sources. Why, then, deny the reality of a woman for that reason? "Only," she writes, "when I was able to broaden my definition of rhetoric and its practice, only when I was able to give Aspasia the kind of acceptance I had always given Socrates, did I realize that I had discovered a pocket of rhetorical activity" (11).

The term *activity* is worth dwelling upon. Rather than regarding the paternalistic narrative of Aspasia as a fixed historical record, which made it difficult for Glenn to move beyond writing a "descriptive, somewhat solitary account" (Glenn 1997, 10) of her subject, she came to view her work as a feminist rhetorician and historian as performative—as an enactment of the field in a different way, to new ends. Indeed, repurposing is served by replacing a view of scholarly or institutional structures as fixed entities with an understanding of them as enacted—and therefore alterable.

By attending to her own rhetorical purposes and to her enactment of them, Glenn composes a feminist methodology that provides a cultural and relational account of Aspasia. In so doing, Glenn rewrites a narrative that renders Aspasia "self-indulgent, licentious, immoral" (1997, 39) to create one that casts her as an actor, navigating her contradictory status as an educated woman, foreigner, and lover of Pericles in order to locate the intellectual and political agency available to her. Glenn's repurposing of Aspasia is just one example of a greater body of work that opens new practices of and purposes for rhetorical scholarship by questioning habitual narratives and practices, imagining ways to appropriate and alter normative conventions, and enacting alternatives that expand and repurpose rhetorical work. As I'll show in the chapters ahead, locating agency remains a rhetorical concern for marginalized subjects even two thousand years later, in our contemporary neoliberal climate. These examples offer us ways to imagine how agency can be claimed even in the face of constraints.

REPURPOSING AVAILABLE MEANS AND RHETORICAL AIMS

I turn now to another repurposing project in feminist rhetoric, which begins by recasting Aristotle's articulation of rhetoric as the "discovery of the available means of persuasion." By titling their collection *Available Means: An Anthology of Women's Rhetoric(s)*, Joy Ritchie and Kate Ronald at once embrace and depart from Aristotle's definition, noting that their decision "reflects our desire to locate women squarely within rhetoric but also to acknowledge that their presence demands that rhetoric be reconceived." (Ritchie and Ronald 2001, xvii). As with Glenn's work on Aspasia, Ritchie and Ronald initiate their repurposing efforts by illuminating the habitual or normative— in this case, that rhetorical participation as framed by Aristotle assumes the "right to speak in the first place" and, more foundationally, "the right to personhood and selfhood" (xvii). As Ritchie and Ronald observe, for women well into the twentieth century, a central task of rhetorical invention involved discovering how to claim the right to speak and, often, to insist upon their right to "personhood and selfhood." This means that women's rhetoric will often sound different than the self-assured, strident voices that have long defined the tradition.

One of their tasks as anthology editors is to help readers employ a practice Andrea Lunsford describes as essential to feminist rhetorical studies: listening hard (Lunsford 1995, 6). And, I would add, listening differently, because the sounds of women's rhetoric—and the scholarship that engages it—have not been traditionally deemed "rhetorical." In fact, Ritchie and Ronald acknowledge that some of the writing in the collection may seem "less than eloquent" (Ritchie and Ronald

2001, xvii). In so doing, they nudge readers to rethink naturalized notions of rhetorical "eloquence," which feature repetitions of linear, logic-driven arguments and bold individual voices, to instead listen deeply for meaningful disruptions and new rhetorical recurrences.

Their anthology gathers voices from the fifth century BCE to 1999, nodding to the convention of building a tradition vis-à-vis individual contributors; but they also repurpose this practicing by listening across and between the texts, as well as to the context surrounding them, to make rhetorical recurrences audible. Both kinds of listening—to individual voices and to recurrences in the collective—are key to repurposing the tradition, but here we see that as scholars located more voices, ripples in the water became waves—more discernable patterns that other rhetors could discern, deploy, and alter. For instance, Ritchie and Ronald call attention to rhetorical patterns that emerge when we look at contributions made by communities of women, both actual (as in Shirley Wilson Logan's 1999 "We are Coming": The Persuasive Discourse of Nineteenth Century Black Women, Jacqueline Jones Royster's 2000 Traces of a Stream: Literacy and Social Change among African American Women, and Anne Ruggles Gere's 1997 Intimate Practices: Literacy and Cultural Work in US. Women's Clubs, 1880–1920) and created, by placing women's words from across historical moments in conversation with one another. The collective voices in Available Means, for instance, demonstrate patterns that move the topoi of rhetoric away from the public sphere and into the kitchen, the diary, the body; expand the range of forms and strategies considered rhetorical; and repeatedly attend to difference within seemingly singular categories.

Read as a collective, these texts demonstrate a pattern of doing rhetoric differently, of enacting it in new way. Even as Ritchie and Ronald gather and anthologize these women's voices, they argue that women's rhetorics are "fluid rather than fixed" (Ritchie and Ronald 2001, xvi). This is the kind of tension with which repurposing efforts require us to grapple; we can at once engage an anthologized collection of women's voices as sanctioned members of the rhetorical tradition and at the same time regard them as dynamic and active, creating opportunities for new directions, meanings, and purposes.

We see a complementary gathering of feminist rhetorical enactment eleven years later in Royster and Kirsch's *Feminist Rhetorical Practices*, which focuses on "feminist-informed operational frameworks[s]" that have emerged from the growing body of scholarship on women's rhetoric. They detect "patterns in motion and patterns of change" in feminist efforts to rescue, recover, and reinscribe rhetoric, which they distill into four "critical terms of engagement": critical imagination, strategic contemplation, social circulation, and globalization (Royster and Kirsch 2012, 19). These tropes that have emerged from feminist rhetorical scholarship, they argue, have acted as "tectonic shifts on the rhetorical landscape" (17) and, they contend, may be (re)enacted to generate new directions and openings.

In both the revisionary acts made by feminist rhetors and in the scholarly practices employed to study them, there are two recurring tactics that I want to highlight as crucial practices for extending acts of repurposing to institutional sites, on which I'll focus in later chapters. The first involves locating and employing as a *resource* that which is typically excised from logical, rationalist modes of knowing, speaking, and writing. We see this trope repeated and extended in women's rhetoric that includes Sojourner Truth's (2001) insistence on her embodiment, as she raises her muscled brown arm to question her audience, "Aren't I a woman?"; Hélène Cixous initiation of *écriture féminine*, a feminine writing practice that embraces uneasiness, questioning, and waste (Cixous 2001, 285); and law professor Patricia Williams's (2001) insistence on story and subjectivity, and herself as an embodied subject, in legal discourse. Similarly, feminist rhetoricians have reclaimed practices often devalued in the classical tradition (and in contemporary culture), evidenced in Glenn's reappropriation of silence as a potentially powerful rhetorical act or Ratcliffe's insistence that cross-cultural communication requires rhetorical listening.

A tactic that works alongside, and sometimes in conjunction with, repurposing "excess" is the employment of conventional rhetorical strategies and values to alternative ends. On such early example is Margaret Fell who, writing in 1666, explicated scripture passages to argue that women should be allowed to speak in church and in public. She offers alternative readings of the words historically used against women and calls attention to passages that underscore the biblical importance of women, reminding readers that that Jesus was "made of a Woman" and that "after his Resurrection [he] also manifested himself unto [women] first of all even before he ascended unto his Father" (Fell 2001, 70). Across women's rhetoric, we see examples of women borrowing from the familiar and valued and altering its purpose so that the practice and constitution of rhetoric is, in effect, remade.

Feminist rhetoricians, too, are cognizant of the balance of working within and against the classical tradition. On the one hand, any kind of disruptive or revisionary practice requires an understanding of how the dominant system functions, but this understanding need not result in dismissal. Understanding the dominant structure can also highlight the potential and possibilities within it. Fell recognized that scripture—even that which seemed damning to women—could also be used to justify women's speech acts. The limitations and possibilities could be held together, and she could then determine how to act based on the range of means available to her. Likewise, in advocating for rhetorical listening, Ratcliffe grounds her work in a discussion of the ancient concept of logos in a manner that not only repurposes listening but also rewrites logos itself.

In the chapters that follow, I build upon the repurposing practices we see deployed in feminist rhetoric and rhetorical studies, showing how they can serve as useful tactics for repurposing our classrooms and institutions. First, though, I turn to parallel repurposing efforts evident in feminist composition and pedagogy scholarship, which offers more insight into how feminist repurposing efforts can break the repetition of our daily institutional lives.

FEMINIST REPURPOSING OF COMPOSITION PEDAGOGY

As with feminist rhetorical studies, feminist scholarship on composition pedagogy did not become a regular, visible presence in the field until the late 1980s. Also like feminist rhetoric, there are material reasons for this. Because composition instruction has historically been characterized as a maternal, service-oriented activity, women have traditionally done, and continue to do, the lion's share of composition teaching, often at the expense of research time (ADE Ad Hoc Committee on Staffing 2008). In fact, early discussions of composition instruction show that the feminization of composition was presumed to reflect a "natural" match between task and subject. In her 1924 article "Academic Status of Women on University Faculties," Ella Lonn reported that English department chairs frequently indicated that "women do a better job of routine work, such as freshman composition, than men, as they are 'painstaking, conscientious, and enthusiastic.'" (Lonn 1924, 8). And "in positions of low salary, involving much drudgery," women were assumed to "do better than men, but solely because they are more nearly tied to the business of teaching than men" (8). In 1930 Stith Thompson offered this comment on the Taylor report: "[Women instructors] do often seem to be willing to settle down to a life of efficient freshman teaching without any idea of going further in their academic career" (quoted in Connors 1990, 121). A significant task for feminists within the field, then, was—and remains—to unearth and reshape normative assumptions about the feminized role of writing instruction.

Just as feminist rhetoricians found women's contributions to the rhetorical tradition outside of the traditional public sphere, Ritchie and Kathleen Boardman remind us that feminist work was present in "informal conversations, in basement classrooms, and in committees on which women served" long before it appeared in journals (Ritchie and Boardman 1999, 8). Beginning in the 1970s, a few feminist voices begin to emerge in the field's scholarship, with the most notable surge arriving after the 1988 publication of Elizabeth Flynn's "Composing as a Woman." This crescendo of contributions has built, now, to a strong, vital presence in the field that features its own repetitions and recurrences.

Ritchie and Boardman (1999) offer one overview of the tropes of feminist composition scholarship, categorizing them as inclusion, metonymy (or an implicit overlap of composition and feminist approaches), and disruption of hegemonic narratives. They are careful to insist that these are neither distinct nor linear, evolutionary tropes, but that distilling them allows for examination of recurrences and patterns in feminist work. They examine each trope in historical context, pointing to both its potential and its limitations. An early example of the inclusion trope, for instance, came in the 1972 "Open Letter from Janet Emig, Chairwoman, NCTE Committee on the Role and Image of Women," which called for nominations to the committee and for testimonies of discrimination. Here, Emig sought both to include women in the landscape of the field and to illuminate the considerably unequal terrain that women navigated in academic life. These narratives were also highlighted in two special issues of *College English*, published in 1971 and 1972, which raised issues ranging from working conditions for women to the absence of women in curricula and pedagogy (Ohmann 1971; Hedges 1972b). The "inclusion" trope might be read as parallel to that of "gender recovery" in feminist rhetorical studies; while it brought crucial attention to women's voices and perspectives, it did not yet disrupt the normative contexts that contributed to women's exclusion in the first place. Indeed, as I'll show in chapter 4, this dynamic remains an issue in contemporary neoliberal contexts, where an ethos of "corporate multiculturalism" may prompt universities to recruit members of marginalized populations and tout the numbers represented in their faculty and student body, but does not disrupt or alter the institutional climate and structures that contributed to their exclusion in the first place (Jones and Calafell 2012, 965).

The second, metonymic trope involves an implicit connection between feminism and the "revisionist writing theory" that arose in the 1970s. As Ritchie and Boardman note, "Emerging pedagogical theories spoke a language that resonated with

feminism's concerns of the time: coming to voice and consciousness, illuminating experience and its relationship to individual
identity, playing the believing game rather than the doubting
game, collaborating rather than competing, subverting hierarchy in the classroom" (Ritchie and Boardman 1999, 14). While
making connections to a more predominant discourse might
have allowed feminists to legitimize their practices, Ritchie and
Boardman point out that this strategy risks obscuring feminist
departures from expressivist approaches to writing. For instance,
while Flynn observes that the process-oriented pedagogies of
the 1970s and 1980s replaced the "figure of an authoritative
father with an image of a nurturing mother," (Flynn 1988, 423),
women experience the naturalized requirement to nurture
in complex ways, as many negative as positive. Therefore, it
became necessary for feminist scholars to highlight their work
against the field's dominant narratives, which brings us to the
disruption trope.

The idea of challenging or disrupting norms is perhaps
the trope most commonly associated with feminism. Feminist
disruption is often associated with anger—as my undergraduate students, who still tend to think of feminism as an angry
enterprise, remind me. And indeed, some of the early work
on feminism in composition points to anger about exclusion,
unequal pay, and unequal treatment as an impetus for disrupting the status quo. This is *not*, as Elaine Hedges writes in 1972,
anger "directed so much against men (a dead-end procedure),
as towards further liberation for the woman writer, critic, and
reader as well. It is an anger that should lead to fresh insights;
new readings of texts, new illuminations of the lives of past
women writers, the rediscovery of women writers who have
been neglected and ignored" (Hedges 1972a, 2). Disruption
(and here, recasting of emotion as a resource—a topic I address
in chapter 2), then, is a tool to illuminate the problems in the
status quo, to create space for new inclusions, and to break patterns of exclusionary practice. While earlier disruptive essays in
the field relied heavily on experiential narratives, contemporary
feminists employ cultural analysis and post-structuralist theory

to disrupt singular assumptions about gender and to open space for new categories of difference, calling attention to linkages among gender, race, class, sexual orientation, and language usage. While it's easy, as Ritchie and Boardman note, to read disruption as the most progressive feminist trope, disruption alone is not sufficient for change—particularly if disruption is disconnected from material conditions and lived experience (Ritchie and Boardman 1999, 22). As Hedges observes of articulations of anger, disruption must not only critique but also invent; it must lead to new, more inclusive practices and ways of enacting our field, our teaching, our writing.

While isolating each of these tropes is extremely useful—allowing greater visibility of the strategies and tactics employed by feminists to revise the field—I argue that repurposing involves a nexus of all three. It brings together inclusion, attention to common ground, and disruption so as to create something new, a result each practice on its own may not achieve. I turn now to several examples from feminist composition pedagogy scholarship that engage all three tropes at once: they illuminate and disrupt business as usual; they examine overlapping goals with dominant discourses, while also attending to differences; and, ultimately, they seek to enact new—more inclusive—possibilities and purposes.

REPURPOSING THE WRITING CLASSROOM

Early scholarship in feminist composition and pedagogy can certainly be read in metonymic relationship with expressivist approaches. In fact, Carolyn Ericksen Hill (1990) provides a retrospective account of composition scholarship in the 1960s and 1970s that theorizes male figures like Peter Elbow, Ken Macrorie, John Schultz, and William Coles Jr. as "midwives" who sponsored a feminine approach to composition pedagogy. Even so, I would argue that early feminist scholars in composition also wrote out of their own scholarly purposes and exigencies, which can be read as related to but still distinct from expressivism.

For instance, feminist pieces like Florence Howe's 1971 "Identity and Expression: A Writing Course for Women" and Pamela J. Annas's 1985 "Style as Politics: A Feminist Approach to the Teaching of Writing" can be viewed as overlapping with practices of consciousness-raising that occurred outside of the academy and its burgeoning women's studies programs. While consciousness-raising is often downplayed even in feminist history—deemed untheoretical or overly focused on the individual—the practice enabled women to understand the normative as gendered, to view individual experience as necessarily shaped by cultural expectations. For this reason, consciousness-raising represents what Megan Boler describes as a "radical turning point" in transforming gender consciousness, even as it is often denigrated and ignored (Boler 1999, 109). She fears, in fact, that by ignoring the role of early feminist practices like consciousness-raising, feminists risk contributing to their own erasure.

To counter this possibility, I highlight how, within composition pedagogy scholarship, this emergent feminist knowledge and practice helped feminist teachers and scholars to repurpose their writing classrooms in order to facilitate the learning of women students. In addition, read alongside expressivist texts, essays like Howe's and Annas's also complicate expressivism, pointing to the importance of gender in how we experience pedagogy. For instance, Howe complicates generic or universal notions of "student writers" by describing the "alleged inferiority" many of her female students experience as they compose. She creates a pedagogy, then, that helps them to see that this experienced inferiority stems not from biology but from "centuries of belief in their inferiority, as well as from male-dominated and controlled institutions" (Howe 1971, 863). While subsequent scholarship would challenge generalized assumptions about women as a singular category, articles like Howe's represent an important move toward approaching the writing classroom as gendered—a line of inquiry not evident in most expressivist and process-based writing scholarship at the time. In so doing, this feminist work insists on the inclusion of women's perspectives in composition scholarship and disrupts perceptions of classrooms or institutional space as gender neutral.

Annas's "Style as Politics" provides a clear example of feminist repurposing of the writing classroom, as it takes into account both the requirements writers face in the academy and looks toward other possibilities for writing. Like the feminists who preceded her, Annas begins by attending to the gendered contexts in which women write. In fact, she grounds her exigency in her own writing and teaching life: "My interest in the politics of style begins in two immediate personal concerns: my own efforts to write as a woman who is both a feminist and an academic and who therefore wants to reach more than one audience, and my work in writing classes with women students who are trying to find an authentic and effective writing voice in classroom situations, for an audience, in the context of approved models that often seem puzzling and alien to them." In so doing, she enacts a form of writing pedagogy that moves beyond valuing the "abstract, logical, and impersonal" at the expense of "sensual, contextual, and committed language" (Annas 1985, 360). This normative approach further sets out, she notes, to "wean" students from more experiential-based writing into seemingly "objective" prose, which is deemed more valuable and rigorous. Ultimately, she moves to dislodge these boundaries, arguing for an approach that is "rigorous without sacrificing subjectivity" (361). As do many feminist rhetors, she embraces as a resource that which is habitually exiled, in this case refusing a boundary between "rigorous" and "personal."

To locate writing possibilities that reach beyond predetermined categories, she and her students look to strategies employed by female essayists. Here, Annas describes writing that finds a "delicate resolution between hostile elements" (Annas 1985, 365–366); that is, Annas aims to help her students consider how writers hold in tension seemingly contradictory purposes and expectations that play out among writer, subject, convention, and audience. How have these writers found a way to both engage and depart from expectations for writers and for women?

While the students may glean strategies from these published writers, they must also take into account their own contexts as writers. So in addition to reading writers such as Virginia Woolf, Gloria Anzaldúa, Adrienne Rich, and Judy Syfer, Annas invites her students to study their own composing processes, noting what facilitates and inhibits their writing. Annas finds that she has some students who have well internalized how to produce the kind of prose that is valued in the academic setting but that also tend to take few risks and to sound "passionless" and generic. She has other students who write for themselves in journals or other "private forms," but who are not apt to share or revise their writing (Annas 1985, 368). Annas admits she is describing two extremes, but her aim to is to bring these two sides together, disrupting distinctions between "subjectivity" and "objectivity" and private and public writing. It is, in fact, to create a new purpose for writing that embraces subjectivity and commitment and at the same time reaches a public audience. To do so, Annas assigns students a position paper based on a topic of "intense interest" to them, whose arguments are to be made equally from "lived experience" and from "more conventional sources of information" (369). The assignment, therefore, works within traditional academic conventions (relying on a persuasive form that employs conventional research) as well as against normative modes (requiring a committed stance and relying on the self as a vital source of information). Ultimately, then, she names a new purpose for writing: "The kind of writing I finally want these students to be able to do brings together the personal and the political, the private and the public, into writing which is committed and powerful because it takes risks, because it speaks up clearly in their own voices and from their experience, experiments with techniques of argumentation and skillful organization, and engages, where appropriate, with the insights of other writers" (370). Annas notes that her female students require support in this process of risk taking and breaking the habitual. She further points out that creating new purposes for writing also means the product has to be valued differently. But composition teachers, she argues, are in a "powerful position" to judge writing based on extended definitions of "good and effective" writing, and to "transfer that sense of possibility" to students (371). While Annas relies on some essentialist notions of women's experience, she disrupts the repetition of the habitual by showing how normative modes of expository writing exclude important modes of knowledge making. She then moves to create opportunities for writing that work at once within and against conventions to create possibilities for wider purposes and subjects.

We see recurrences of this approach in subsequent scholarship in the field, which includes and reaches beyond the category of gender to consider how social locations like sexual orientation (Herrington and Curtis 2000; Malinowitz 1995), class (LeCourt and Napoleone 2011; Soliday 1999), race (Gilyard 1999; Villanueva 1993; Villanueva and Smitherman 2003), and translingualism (Lu and Horner 2013) shape students' experience of academic writing and the writing classroom. They remind us that privileged language practices reflect "the cultural preferences of the most powerful people in the community" (Bizzell 2002b, 1), but that despite descriptors like "standard English," they are not fixed or singular. By illuminating and disrupting normative assumptions about academic writing, this body of work helps us to think about how we can help students to both succeed within and discover possibilities beyond the habitual. As Bizzell contends, alternative discourses "allow their practitioners to do intellectual work in ways they could not if confined to traditional academic discourse. These new discourses enable scholarship to take account of new variables, to explore new methods, and to communicate findings in new venues, including broader reading publics than the academic" (Bizzell 2002b, 3). As I'll demonstrate in the chapters ahead, this practice of repurposing academic writing is particularly crucial at a time when there is pressure to view writing primarily as a tool to be used in the workplace—a product to serve an economic end.

REPURPOSING WRITING SUBJECTS

The role of the writing teacher constitutes another crucial site of feminist repurposing in composition scholarship. It is not surprising that this role would garner recurrent feminist attention, since it has been subject to external cultural and institutional pressures in ways few other disciplines experience. As Sharon Crowley observes, "Composition is administered and taught in a much thicker discursive network than are other academic courses" (Crowley 1998, 259). Analyzing that discursive network, which functions reciprocally with material conditions, is the first step of repurposing.

Sue Ellen Holbrook's 1988 Conference on College Composition and Communication presentation "Women's Work: The Feminizing of Composition" functioned as a catalyst for inquiry into how and why the composition teacher is feminized, and how this normative conception is at once repeated and overlooked. Holbrook's study evidenced the literal feminization of the field at the time, when two-thirds of all who taught composition were female; but she also pointed to the low, feminized status of composition teaching, associating it with service-based pedagogy rather than knowledge-producing theory (Holbrook 1988, 9). While feminists in composition would continue to survey the gender divisions and material conditions for women in the field (Enos 1997; Miller 1991; Schell 1997), they also extended the study to consider the "discursive network" surrounding composition students, teachers, and classrooms.

Susan Miller's 1991 *Textual Carnivals: The Politics of Composition* and Sharon Crowley's 1998 *Composition in the University* provide histories that—much like Glenn's work with ancient rhetoric—reveal how a feminized, service status became conflated with the writing teacher. As Crowley argues, composition instruction is built upon a discourse of students' needs—emerging from both outside and within the institution—and, by extension, expectations about what teachers must do and be in order to meet these needs. The discourse of need grows louder during moments of perceived crisis, from Harvard students in

1873 failing a written entrance exam to the contemporary economic crises that demands better-prepared workers.

Crowley argues that this discursive network defines students as passive consumers of pedagogy determined *for* them, not with them (Crowley 1998, 260). Teachers are also denied agency in this discursive network, subject to external definitions of their roles, too often denied a voice in the curriculum they are expected to teach. Because composition teachers are often relegated to the margins of university structures, Crowley contends that it is not unusual for teachers to internalize the discourse of need, which then becomes an "ethic of service." Drawing from feminist philosopher Nancy Fraser, Crowley notes that members of subordinate groups may adopt others' "need interpretations that work to their own disadvantage" (262).

We see a similar critique in Miller's examination of the "female coding" of the composition teacher. In addition to noting the statistical evidence of the field's feminization, Miller advocates for highlighting the feminized *ideological construction* of the composition teacher, which ties the writing teacher to "fantasized functions and activities" more than to her actual situation (Miller 1991, 123). While one of the fantasized functions of the writing teacher is that of maternity, Miller articulates a more complex role. To do so, she points to the nineteenth-century mother and maid, whose roles involved both comfort and power, as she educated, nurtured, and disciplined the children (137). Similarly, the composition teacher cleans and "cures" the young language user of discursive ills, a task that requires both care and discipline, as she readies the writer for more important work beyond the realm of the composition classroom. Miller writes, "This teacher must represent established means of discriminating and evaluating students . . . [she] must also be the culture to which the student is introduced" (138). The teacher's authority, then, is relative to the degree to which she *enacts* the values and practices that are sanctioned by her cultural and/or institutional context—much in the way that Crowley suggests a teacher may gain authority by adopting the institution's discourse of need.

By framing the discursive network that shapes conceptions of composition teachers and students through a gendered lens, Crowley and Miller lay the groundwork for repurposing these roles. In fact, both insist that our conceptions of the composition teacher will not change until we rethink constructions of students as "presexual, preeconomic, prepolitical" subjects (Miller 1991, 192) whose needs are externally determined. This charge is resonant in our contemporary culture, in which students are often defined as customers whose decisions are based solely on the market. As Elizabeth Brulé writes, "De-sexed, de-faced, de-classed and able-bodied, it is assumed that that the student as a consumer can and will make economically rational choices" (2004, 255). In both cases, then, students' complexity remains obscured.

While redefining understandings of student writers is a discipline-wide enterprise, feminist scholars have trained a keen eye on how these articulations—including those with liberatory or feminist claims—may reify normative, masculinist assumptions for both students and teachers. First published the same year as Miller's 1991 *Textual Carnivals*, for instance, Susan Jarratt's oft-cited "Feminism and Composition: The Case for Conflict" offers a parallel critique of the teacher as nurturer and seeks to repurpose the role of teacher and student. Rather than examining problematic articulations of students and teachers from outside the field, however, Jarratt focuses on a position she views as shared by both composition and feminism: "a strong resistance to conflict." Her concern is that a privileging of harmony prohibits examination and disruption of power dynamics in the classroom, placing the teacher in the position of creating a nurturing and "safe" environment. Her concern is that the requirement to create and sustain a nurturing environment that elides conflict has the potential to reify existing social relations for female teachers and students alike. Jarratt observes, "[Elbow's] *Writing Without Teachers* is truly a revolutionary text in its feminization of the male writing teacher. But female readers—teachers or students of composition—are positioned differently in relation to these instructions" (Jarratt 2003, 268). For women, then, the

directive to "listen openly and acceptingly" to every utterance in
the classroom may function as an echo of the cultural prescrip-
tion for female behavior: self-sacrificing, supportive, silent.

Jarratt does not end with a disruption of the habitual in contemporary writing pedagogies; she also offers something new.
This "something new," however, is a result of repurposing other
practices and theories, including those she critiques. As she
writes, "It's not a question of throwing out the innovations of
teachers like Elbow and Murray or of shutting down the voices
and personal experiences of students; rather, it's a question
of relocating those practices and interests in a different theoretical context" (2003, 270). The theoretical context in which
Jarratt relocates—and thus repurposes—those innovations is
built from feminist critical pedagogy and sophistic rhetoric.
From the feminist critical pedagogy of bell hooks and Kathleen
Weiler, she calls attention to subjectivity and personal experience examined through a social and historical lens. At the same
time, Jarratt contends that contemporary composition pedagogy can benefit from the sophistic tradition of placing *dissoi
logoi*—conflicting views about an issue—at the center of rhetorical practice (271). Jarratt argues for writing courses based on
a "rhetorical composition theory" that merges the private and
public, that engages both lived experience and public writing.
As she writes, "I envision a composition course in which students
argue about ethical implications of discourse on a wide range
of subjects and, in so doing, come to identify their personal
interests with others, understand those interests as implicated
in a larger communal setting, and advance them in a public
voice" (277). By fusing feminist pedagogy and sophistic rhetoric,
Jarratt articulates a revised purpose of a composition classroom.

This pedagogy argues, as do many feminist pedagogies
emerging at this moment, that roles for teachers and students
are best determined by subjects situated in particular, local contexts. While the local and embodied elements of institutional
life are often considered "excessive" to what is most valued—
abstract, efficient, standardized knowledge—feminists advocate for these considerations as necessary to rhetorically sound,

context-sensitive pedagogies. Rather than relying on fixed roles, feminist pedagogy increasingly calls for fluidity and flexibility of these positions, depending on who is in the classroom, how power differentials function among students and between teachers and students, and how these subjectivities intersect with the cultural moment and institutional contexts. The teacher is not a fixed maternal figure, a neutral fellow writer, or a master rhetor; she may occupy any one of these roles, or all of them, or move within and among them to suit the rhetorical moment and her students in it.

For this reason, a growing number of feminist scholars call for a rhetorical approach to the pedagogies teachers perform that is based on the local context, exigency, power dynamics, and subjects involved (Jung 2005; Kopelson 2006; LeCourt and Napoleone 2011). Julie Jung puts it this way:

> The knowledge that pedagogical performance is a rhetorical choice rather than the "natural" consequence of identity (Feminist Teacher) challenges universalist claims about how feminists and other oppositional teachers "should" teach. Rather than begin with claims to identity, a strategy that repeatedly offered me nothing but binary options, I can instead foreground my feminist-motivated pedagogical purpose . . . With this goal in mind, I can redefine teaching "styles"—i.e., nurturing, traditional, and confrontational—as performance genres and generate disruption by self-consciously juxtaposing them within the classroom space. (Jung 2005, 147)

Of course, this does not mean that the teacher is in full control of her performance, or that she can finally control how students read her. As LeCourt and Napoleone contend, "How [our] performances are read . . . depends much upon the particularities of the academic social spaces in which we are located and the power differentials among the actors in those spaces" (LeCourt and Napoleone 2011, 87). This approach does, however, disrupt ideas that there is a "right" way to enact a feminist classroom to instead emphasize the importance of kairos—taking into account rhetorical circumstances and contingencies including audience, social dynamics, message, and timing to choose the most effective way to communicate.

Just as feminist rhetors make room for multiplicity, inclusion, and agency, so, too, do feminist scholars in composition pedagogy create room for more ways of inhabiting the classroom and for multiple purposes for writing and writing instruction. At this moment when the value of writing classrooms is increasingly tied to neoliberal purposes, feminist approaches offer ways to hold multiple, even seemingly contradictory, purposes together. The both/and approach that is integral to feminist repurposing allows us to consider how we can take seriously our students' material needs for job readiness as well as to highlight and enact the feminist ideas that may otherwise be obscured in the neoliberal university.

In the chapters ahead, I focus on terms that represent key tensions between neoliberal and feminist views: *emotion, listening, agency,* and *responsibility.* I argue that feminist thought enables a repurposing of these terms and their enactment so as to allow for more expansive possibilities and purposes for teaching and learning. Next, then, I turn to discussions of emotion and "emotional intelligence" in the neoliberal university, considering how feminist repurposing of emotion helps us to think beyond a discourse of emotional management to one that views emotion as a rich (and rational) resource for knowledge.

NOTES

1. My use of the term *tactic* follows Michel de Certeau's conception. De Certeau views tactics as the purview of the marginalized, who work within and against existing conditions to create new possibilities or outcomes. He offers the example of *los indio* (indigenous people in Central and South America) using tactics in the context of Spanish colonization: "The Indians often used the laws, practices, and representations that were imposed on them by force or by fascination to ends other than those of their conquerors; they made something else out of them; they subverted them from within" (de Certeau 1984, 32).

2. While some of the texts I read as examples of "feminist repurposing" chronologically precede the concept of feminism, I categorize their rhetorical efforts as such because their values, arguments, and aims disrupt normative categories of gender, call for greater inclusion, and argue for or enact new possibilities. I view these moves as part of the feminist project.

2

FEMINIST REPURPOSING OF EMOTION

From Emotional Management to Emotion as Resource

In a 2011 *Huffington Post* education column, Alicia Morga describes the usual culprits deemed responsible for school failure, including unions, ill-prepared teachers, and insufficient budgets. She has her own theory, however, about why education is "broken": "The root of our failing education system from K–12 all the way though college is lack of one basic skill: the ability to manage our emotions" (Morga 2011). Drawing upon the research of Daniel Goleman (1995), the author of the *New York Times* best-seller *Emotional Intelligence: Why It Can Matter More than IQ*,[1] she argues that students who fail to "identify, appropriately express, and manage" emotion face consequences ranging from reduced academic achievement scores to lack of job success. The remedy, Morga argues, is curriculum—taught in every year of school through adulthood—that aids development of "emotional skills." After all, she contends, students and adults will be effective learners and workers only when "their emotional concerns are addressed and managed" (Morga 2011).

Morga's assessment of emotion as a renegade force, in need of discipline and control, speaks to larger cultural definitions of emotion as an impediment to rationalism and productivity. The argument follows, then, that for the sake of educational and economic success, we need to produce more emotionally "intelligent" subjects who are able to harness and manage emotion, exhibiting strong regulation and emotional restraint. Indeed, businesses have latched onto emotional intelligence discourse to train employees and sponsor managerial leadership. In fact, its advocates deem this brand of emotional literacy "vital in every aspect of life—for successful relations, for achieving your

DOI: 10.7330/9781607323884.c002

full potential and for career stardom" (McWilliam and Hatcher 2004, 180). Or as *Time* magazine puts it, "IQ may get you hired but EQ [emotional intelligence quotient] gets you promoted" (quoted in Boler 1999, 93).

The management of emotions is valorized inside the academy as well. For instance, in a cross-disciplinary, four-year study of faculty and students' assumptions about writing, Chris Thaiss and Terry Myers Zawacki distilled three generally agreed-upon characteristics of academic writing. Two of the three underscore the import of "rationalism"; one features the role of the writer, who is expected to display "the dominance of reason over emotion or sensual perception," and the other addresses the implied reader, who is assumed to be "coolly rational, reading for information, and intending to formulate a reasoned response" (Thaiss and Zawacki 2006, 5–7). Like the emotionally intelligent subject who controls emotion with rationality, "disciplined" academic subjects display a subjugation of emotion to reason.

Given the entrenched assumptions about emotion—disorderly, irrational, corporeal—it isn't surprising that it has historically been associated with women. As Megan Boler highlights, within educational institutions, unacceptable or seemingly negative emotion is defined by what (or whom) it is not: "namely, the prototype of the rational, curious, engaged, 'balanced,' well behaved white male student" (Boler 1999, 140). However, as she further contends, *discussion* of emotion is typically silenced (140), muting opportunities to examine the institutional and cultural assumptions that inform predominant views of emotion—a move that further solidifies normative conceptions.

This chapter aims to make audible a discussion of emotion[2], showing how feminists have both illuminated and challenged normative understandings of emotion and repurposed it as a site for resistance, inquiry, and new knowledge and writing practices. Here, rather than managing emotion as a means of containment, I argue for engaging it through a process of reflection and critical inquiry. In what follows, I first explore dominant cultural tropes of emotion and show how they operate in the emotional intelligence movement that influences both corporate and educational settings. Here, emotion is deemed a private response that is legitimate so long as it is disciplined and controlled by rationalism. Then, I move to feminist (re)articulations of emotion, which dislodge the repeated characterization of emotion as private, renegade, and irrational. I go on to argue for a pedagogy that repurposes emotion as a cultural discourse and facilitates examination of how social and cultural factors shape the ways we respond (emotionally) to others' words and views. By examining how our emotions have been schooled and how and why we respond emotionally to the world, we gain an opportunity for deeper reflection and insight. As Laura Micciche argues, "Without a framework for understanding emotion's legitimate role in the making of meaning and in the creation of value in our culture, we impoverish our own and our students' understanding of how we come to orient ourselves to one another and to the world around us" (2007, 1). The goal, then, is not to create subjects who contain or excise emotion but to facilitate the repurposing of emotion as a resource for knowledge.

To argue for this pedagogy, I show how we can use public texts—in this case, media responses to emotion portrayed by Barack Obama and Hillary Clinton—to unearth and challenge naturalized conceptions of emotion. I then move on to the text of my classroom, examining how we might repurpose emotions from something to be controlled to a generative part of intellectual, rhetorical work. Doing so, I argue, allows us to recognize and value students as emotional *and* intellectual subjects.

ARISTOTLE, COGNITIVISM, AND EMOTIONAL INTELLIGENCE

Discussions of emotion and rhetoric date back to Aristotle, whose notion of moral anger joins beliefs and reason in his contention that an analysis of emotions' origins allows one to potentially render them for public good. For instance, in this oft-quoted dictum, Aristotle argues, "Anyone who does not get angry in the right way at the right time and with the right people, is a dolt." For Aristotle, anger is a right response when one's honor or dignity has been challenged, which can then lead to appropriate action. While Greek epistemology did not absolutely separate reason from emotion, reason was privileged above emotion as the controlling agent. Further, as feminists like Boler (1999) and Elizabeth Spelman (1989) argue, the anger to which Aristotle refers is a (privileged) man's anger, not the anger of a woman and not the anger of a male slave. Anger is authorized only for those subjects already deemed rational, subjects who can presumably discipline emotion with reason.

While feminist scholars disagree about the extent to which Aristotle's notion of emotion can be appropriated for contemporary projects that aim to value emotion alongside reason,[3] most agree that classical rhetoric is often *employed* in ways that reinforce a reason/emotion binary. One such example is found in Gretchen Flesher Moon's study of twenty-five rhetoric textbooks published after 1998. She notes that despite the flourishing research on emotion in composition and rhetoric, textbooks—one of the major ways we document and promote teaching in the field—offer limited and often reductive treatment of emotion as part of rhetorical work. If addressed at all, emotion is referenced only in terms of pathos, a persuasive appeal to the emotion of the listener/reader (Moon 2003, 35). Even then, emotional appeal is often deemed unsavory and less effective than logos, the appeal to logic.

For instance, in his popular rhetorical text *Thank You for Arguing*, Jay Heinrichs proposes that if arguments were children, pathos would be "the sibling the others disrespect but who gets away with everything" (Heinrichs 2008, 40). Pathos is in need of discipline. Indeed, Heinrichs goes on to instruct that successful deployment of pathos depends on "self-control" (82); appealing to or arousing others' emotions is more effective when the speaker appears emotionally neutral. Emotion, then, is deemed acceptable when a "rational" subject deploys it as a tool rather than when a speaker or writer presumably *feels* it.

The deployment of emotion in these textbooks illustrates the predominant philosophical frameworks for understanding emotion: positivism and cognitivism. Positivism is associated with a scientific distinction between natural fact and human values, which are perceived as emotional and subjective, and thus rendered a threat to reason (Jaggar 1989). The positivist approach regards emotion as "dumb" (Spelman 1989), an internal and private response restricted to the body. Far more predominant from the late twentieth century onward is cognitivist theory, which offers a vision of emotion that is closer to Aristotle's. Here emotion is inseparable from belief and reason; it assumes that there is always a contextual reason for an emotion, such that an emotion is always "about" something" (Spelman 1989). Consequently, cognitivism ties emotion to judgment and divides it into two parts: an affective or feeling component and a cognitive interpretation or identification of the emotion (Jaggar 1989). However, this does not mean the two components are equally valued. As Worsham puts it, "Cognitivism works indirectly on emotion, which remains 'dumb,' through reason" (Worsham 1998, 224).

While feminist thinkers, among others, have critiqued cognitivism for its stubborn distinction between intellect and affect, cognitivism remains a dominant cultural pedagogy of emotion. As I show above, this is demonstrated in the emotional intelligence movement, which is characterized by five main traits: (1) knowing one's emotions, which gives one a greater sense of control; (2) managing emotions, the ability to "shake off" negative emotions; (3) motivating oneself, including delaying gratification and stifling impulses; (4) recognizing emotion in others; and (5) handling relationships, or "skill in managing emotions in others" (Gardner 1985, 43–44). Here emotion—one's own and others'—is a response in need of managing; it is deemed a personal response that the successful, rationale person is able to overcome.

One factor that makes EQ so marketable in the United States is its status as a "learnable" skill; presumably anyone, given the proper training, can acquire the "proper way to be emotional" (McWilliam and Hatcher 2004, 181). As the "desired traits" indicate, however, particular "emotion skills" are privileged above others—specifically those that lend themselves to corporate values: passion, self-possession, and the ability to work with others (McWilliam and Hatcher 2004). The movement, then, is not so much about valuing emotion as it is about harnessing *particular* emotions so as to produce a subject with "capacity for skills and efficiency as well as . . . good character and rule obedience." (Boler 1999, 59). Boler emphasizes that there is little doubt about the identity of this pedagogy's idealized subject: "The good person is he—and I do mean 'he'—who is taught the right skills to capitalize on the hard wired virtues" (59).

In this age of both neoliberalism and fear of school violence, emotional literacy has also become part of many schools' curricula, often under the general theme of "I am in control of me" (Boler 1999, 91). It is not surprising to see an emphasis on control during a culturally fraught moment; the problem is that too great an emphasis on emotional control can lead to reductive binaries between emotion and rationalism. As Susan Bordo contends, "When the universe becomes unmanageable, human beings become absolutists. We create a world without ambiguity in order to escape, as Dewey puts it, 'from the vicissitudes of experience'" (1987, 17). Consequently, we may seek to avoid the ambiguity and discomfort that accompany genuine inquiry into emotional investments.

Indeed, in Boler's qualitative study of four different emotional literacy curricula in the United States, Australia, and New Zealand, she found that each curriculum emphasized self-control but foregrounded either an individual development model, which teaches impulse-control skills, or a conflict-resolution model, which teaches values such as respect, fairness, helpfulness, and responsibility (1999, 95). Within both of these frameworks, however, Boler discovered that the majority of all classroom instances she observed approached emotion as separate from social contexts and power relations. When individuals are thought to be equally capable of learning skills to monitor and control their emotions, regardless of social contexts, then individuals can also be blamed for lacking skills to self-regulate or control "impulses." In such a formulation, a view of how and why particular subjects have developed social strategies and responses in the contexts of their lives is lost. As a result, it isn't surprising that marginalized groups are often seen as innately "more emotional" than dominant groups.

Consequently, while cognitivism, and the emotional intelligence movement in particular, insists that the proper emotional skills can be taught, it also inadvertently promotes the idea that particular emotional responses, like anger, bitterness, or rage, are urges in need of control rather than social responses to oppression and exploitation. As Worsham puts it, "In general, the dominant pedagogy of emotion refuses the expression of anger by subordinates" and thus "makes it almost impossible to see that sometimes and in some contexts emotions such as anger and bitterness may offer a form of political insight" to a "true source of injury and disappointment" (Worsham 1998, 225).

Despite its shortcomings, however, the emotional intelligence movement does serve us by making emotion a visible part of public discourse. This visibility creates an opportunity for feminist repurposing of emotion as historically, culturally, and socially contingent.

FEMINIST REPURPOSING OF EMOTIONS

Because emotion is typically assigned both a devalued, feminized status and considered the natural province of women, feminist scholars have a clear impetus for repurposing it. One of the first steps in doing so is to illuminate and dislodge the way that women—cast as emotional and irrational beings—are at once deemed repositories and regulators of emotion. Boler writes, "They [women] must embody irrationality (e.g. as the nurturing caregiver, and the embodiment of passions) while simultaneously they are held responsible for 'removing' irrationality from children in order to civilize them" (Boler 1999, 42). This misconception is particularly burdensome to those of us in composition, as I demonstrated in the previous chapter, since composition teachers have long occupied a feminized role in the university, expected to shape students' subjectivity so as

to prepare them for subsequent "real" disciplinary or professional work. For female (and feminized) teachers, this shaping
of student subjectivity has historically involved fostering self-
regulation by removing or controlling irrationality/emotion.
While feminist scholars recognize the centrality of emotion
in subject formation, they aim to disrupt the naturalized conceptions of emotion as individualized, internally located, and
privately experienced. Instead, feminist scholars argue for a
reconception of emotion as a "dominant cultural category" that
shapes the way we experience ourselves and the world (Lutz
1988, 54). Worsham usefully defines emotion as a "tight braid
of affect and judgment, socially and historically constructed and
bodily lived, through which the symbolic takes hold of and binds
the individual, in complex and contradictory ways, to the social
order and its structure of meaning" (Worsham 1998, 216).

With emotions no longer viewed as a "private problem" or
individualized experience, feminist scholars illuminate how they
serve as a primary site for schooling subjectivity, such that we
learn through "gendered rules of emotional conduct" (Boler
1999, xiv) what aspects of ourselves are considered excessive or
shameful. As Worsham contends, "The discourse of emotion is
our primary education, (primary in the sense of both earliest
and foundational)," such that the predominant sites in which we
live and work—family, school, workplace—are all "pedagogies of
emotion" (Worsham 1998, 216). Once we understand emotional
discourse as enacted in a range of public pedagogical sites, there
exists a possibility for disrupting the repetition of how emotion is
taught and for discovering new purposes for emotion.

For instance, while emotions serve as a site of social control,
feminists have long argued that they may also serve as a source
for political resistance. This is another trait of feminist repurposing: reclaiming what has been excised to new ends. This
tactic is evident in Alison Jaggar's use of "outlaw" emotions—
feelings like anger and resentment that are deemed wrong
and denied to marginalized groups. These, she argues, offer
potential, when expressed, to challenge cultural hegemony and
open avenues for social change (Jaggar 1989, 143–149). More

recently, feminist sociologist Brené Brown (2010) has argued for repurposing vulnerability, which our culture deems weak, feminized, and shameful, as the very cornerstone of engagement, courage, and agency. The countercultural message of vulnerability as a resource, something to value and accept rather than to cover and excise, clearly resonates with public audiences: Brown's TEDTalk on the subject went viral and has, at present, nearly 9 million hits. Feminist scholars remind us that when emotion, once locked away in the private realm, is reconceived as social, it emerges as a potentially forceful rhetoric for fostering collective experience and action.

I argue, then, that a first step in repurposing emotion in educational sites requires studying it as a socially composed public text, as rhetoric, with our students. This allows us to develop a way of reading, discussing, and engaging emotion as part of learning, asking the following questions: How do expressions of emotion vary according to cultural norms and contexts? How can we read emotions as social rather than individual or natural? What shapes our understanding of an emotion's appropriateness or usefulness?

EMOTION AS A PUBLIC, POLITICAL TEXT

Although emotions are prominently displayed in U.S. popular culture—from tabloids that aim to catch a celebrity couple in heated argument to reality shows that market contestants' humiliation for ratings—we do not get regular practice in reading emotions as part of a cultural and political landscape. In what follows, I argue for examining public rhetoric of emotion through texts and repurposing practices that help us to (1) make visible the social factors that result in seemingly natural ways of categorizing emotion, and (2) examine the multiple ways emotions are read as appropriate or not when expressed by different subjects and in different contexts.

A compelling example of emotion as public rhetoric occurred when President Barack Obama responded to Wall Street bonuses granted after the federal government bailout. Obama's response,

during which he categorized the bonuses as "the height of irre-
sponsibility" and "shameful," was punctuated with an angry tone
rarely heard from this politician dubbed "No Drama Obama"
for his calm, steady demeanor and rational subjectivity. Obama's
anger quickly became a topic of news coverage, and for the
most part was praised by the mainstream media. As *U.S. News
and World Report* pointed out, the story led all three major network newscasts: "*ABC World News* reported, "The President did
not mince words this afternoon, indeed he was angry.' The
CBS Evening News said the country 'found out what it takes to
get . . . Obama angry,' and *NBC Nightly News* described Obama as
'channeling his inner populist'" (*US News and World Report* 2009).

Moments like these, when emotion becomes a topic of media
coverage, serve as useful public texts through which to open
discussion of emotional epistemologies and how they shape
assumptions about subjectivity. One way to begin a conversation
about the rhetoric of anger, for instance, might involve intro-
ducing students to Jaggar's claim that "while members of subordinate groups are expected to be emotional, their anger will
not be tolerated" (Jaggar 1989, 264). This disregard for marginalized subjects' anger is due to the perceived threat it represents
to those in the dominant group, "not only because the subordinates' anger might be followed up by action, but because it
surely signals that subordinates take themselves seriously; they
believe they have the capacity as well as the right to be judges of
those around them" (267).

Of course, Obama does not fall neatly into one category or
the other—dominant or marginalized, black or white—which
makes the rhetoric of and surrounding his anger even more
ripe for analysis. Why, we might ask, is Obama, whose subject
positions include male, biracial, Ivy League–educated, president, father, heterosexual, upper-class (though from the working class), read, ultimately, as a rational being who can use emotion productively? How might we read this anger differently if
the speaker were a black woman? A white man? While many
media outlets praised Obama's expressed outrage over the Wall
Street raises, other news coverage remarked on the anger as

"contrived" and "calculated," merely a rhetorical performance. This underscores the idea that for Obama, emotion was a mere rhetorical strategy deployed for rational purposes—not something he embodied or "held" innately.

In addition to considering which aspects of Obama's social location seem to "win out" over others, we might also examine how the current political climate informs the way his anger is read and sanctioned. As one media commentator recently pointed out, the American public has shifted its tendency to blame minorities and immigrants for problems in the U.S. economy to Wall Street executives and CEOs, whom they view as greedy and corrupt. Obama's anger at Wall Street execs, which serves to judge and denounce corporate bosses, then, matches a (perceived) public sense of who should be blamed, thereby making it more acceptable. This dynamic is evident as well when later in Obama's presidency, the *Wall Street Journal* chronicled what was headlined "A Brief History of Obama's 'Angry' Moments," which tended to square with public outrage on issues like the BP oil spill, the problems with the healthcare enrollment website, and the mismanagement of Veterans Affairs facilities (Epstein 2014). For Obama, then, public performances of anger are deemed acceptable when they overlap with a larger public sentiment.

Comedians Keegan Michael Key and Jordan Peele, who star in Comedy Central's *Key and Peele* show, offer another perspective on Obama's allowable emotional range, providing commentary on which emotions an African American man may or may not display. After South Carolina congressman Joe Wilson shouted, "You lie" at Obama during the 2009 State of the Union address, Key and Peele created the character Luther, who serves as the "Obama anger translator." They understood that Obama could not risk coming off as an "angry black man," particularly early in his presidency, so Luther reveals what they imagine Obama must suppress. In the "Anger Translator" sketches, Peele delivers a pitch-perfect Obama impersonation, while Key, as Luther, stands to the side, offering emotive commentary peppered with cultural critique:

PEELE: (As Obama) Now, I know a lot of folks say that I haven't done a good job at communicating my accomplishments to the public.

KEY: (As Luther) Because y'all (bleep) don't listen.

PEELE: (As Obama) Since being in office, we've created three million new jobs.

KEY: (As Luther) Three million new jobs.

PEELE: (As Obama) We ended the war in Iraq.

KEY: (As Luther) Ended the war, y'all. We ended a war, remember that?

PEELE: (As Obama) These achievements should serve as a reminder that I am on your side.

KEY: (As Luther) I am not a Muslim.

PEELE: (As Obama) And that my intentions as your president are coming from the right place.

KEY: (As Luther) They're coming from Hawaii, which is where I'm from, which is in the United States of America, y'all, OK? This is ridiculous. I have a birth certificate. I have a birth certificate. I have a hot diggity, daggity, mamase mamasa mamakusa birth certificate you dumb-ass crackers, so . . .

PEELE: (As Obama) OK, Luther, rope it in.

KEY: (As Luther) Yeah, dial it back, Luther, damn.

Luther serves as a way to illuminate what is "unaddressed" both in public discourse and in Obama's measured responses. This is underscored by Luther's response to public scrutiny of Obama's birthplace and religion as well as in what Obama (Peele), in response to Luther, tries to censor:

KEY: (As Luther) And I'm gonna say it right now, mostly white people, stupid. Young white men, 26, get your act together.

PEELE: (As Obama) All right, well, let's rope it in. Let's not make it racial. Let's not make anything racial, ever. (Fresh Air 2013)

The sketches, then, offer sharp criticism of cultural silences about race and also highlight Obama as a figure who is, who must be, always in control of his emotions. As the "angry black man," Luther calls attention to racial discrimination and therefore stands in vivid contrast to the public Obama who displays anger, as in the Wall Street example, when it is publically sanctioned. Key and Peele's Luther skits inevitably lead to Obama's discipline of Luther—telling him to "rope it in" or "dial it back"—showing that Obama can't risk demonstrating outrage about racial discrimination, or about how the public reads his embodied identity.

Public treatments of emotion like the Wall Street example or Key and Peele's skits help us analyze culturally sanctioned and prohibited emotions, but they also serve as potential avenues to examine how we have been schooled to respond to others' emotions. For instance, as my spouse and I watched Obama's remarks on Wall Street delivered on television, my first response was concern. I worried that the shift in his tone from calm to angry might indicate personal strain of the job. In other words, I quickly moved into the position of the emotional caretaker, a response inevitably tied to my own emotional schooling: when a man is upset, you take care of him. My husband, alternatively, read him not as angry but as very "serious," and his response to Obama's sharp tone was minimal. He read it as a strategy for emphasizing the gravity of the situation, not a sign of Obama's inner state.

Since women are often viewed as repositories of emotion, gender plays a significant in role in cultural readings of and responses to emotion. This became clear in the rhetoric surrounding Hillary Clinton's emotions during the 2008 Democratic primaries. The moment under examination occurred when a reporter asked Clinton how she "does it" on the campaign trail, day in and day out. Tears welled in her eyes. "It's not easy. It's not easy," she said. "This is very personal for me. It is not just political. It is not just public. I see what's happening. We have to reverse it. And some people think elections are a game; think like who is up who is down. It's about our country. It's about our kids' future. It's about all of us together. Some of us put ourselves out there and do this against some difficult odds" (quoted in Breslau 2008).

Tellingly, Clinton's tears drew much media coverage, including extensive debate among pundits about whether the tears indicated (female) weakness, human emotion from an often "aloof"-seeming female candidate, or (female) manipulation. Many broadcasts compared this to a 1972 campaign moment when Democratic candidate Ed Muskie got teary over media coverage of his wife. Ultimately, he was deemed weak and unpresidential. When my Rhetoric of Women Writers students and I discussed this moment, we concluded that Clinton's tears evoked a much more fraught response, given that the public grappled not only with the emotional display of a political figure but also with the demonstration of emotions by a candidate who could become the first female president. It may not be surprising, then, as one of my students pointed out, that Clinton's eyes welling with tears for a brief moment soon became a cultural narrative about "Hillary crying." In fact, *Newsweek* reported that even as Clinton spoke, a local TV reporter broadcasted a live report that Clinton "had started crying" (Breslau 2008). Other reporters tried to correct him, but the evocative contradictory image, exaggerated or not, of a woman seeking power *and* crying, proved difficult to shake.

While reporters repeatedly asked Clinton to comment on her "emotional" moment—the campaign explained it as a combination of fatigue, frustration, and emotion—the reported public response is perhaps more telling. For instance, one Fox News pundit accused Clinton of trotting out tears "to remind everyone that she has a womb, that she's a woman, that she's a human being, and look, there are tears in her eyes. She's not the glacier that everyone thinks she is" (Think Progress 2008). And while there was disagreement over whether the tears were genuine, many of those who embraced them as real did, in fact, view them as a sign of humanness. As the *New York Times* reported, "Women, in particular, responded: Several said they chose to vote for Mrs. Clinton at the last moment because she has shown a human side of herself they had never seen" (Healy 2008). Terry McAuliffe, Clinton campaign chair, even attributed Clinton's New Hampshire primary victory, in part, to her emotional display: "Our back was against the wall, but people got to see the real Hillary Clinton," he said. "People saw the contrast of the records in the debate. The humanizing moment she had was a big deal. People know that she'll deliver for them" (quoted in Healy 2008).

Examining the media's rhetoric surrounding Clinton's "teary" moment provided a useful opportunity for my students and me to view emotion as a public text to which we have socially shaped responses. We discussed, for instance, why a politician's emotions become national news. How do we define private versus public lives, and where is emotion accepted or disallowed? While we talked extensively about a female candidate needing to prove that she is not "weak" and thereby not "emotional," we also found it interesting that for many people, Clinton's alleged "aloofness" and extreme professionalism seemed more problematic than did her expression of emotion. In fact, at least according to political analysts, polled women voters seemed to embrace her expression of emotion as a sign of something innately human, or, I would argue, innately feminine. As the Fox News remark demonstrates, her emotional response was read as an indication that she is "a woman," that she has "a womb." This led us to wonder: what was more threatening to cultural expectations, a woman running for office or a woman who seemed emotionally inexpressive? In fact, it seemed that her human—or "feminine"—display of emotions won her significant votes.

Now, as Clinton's 2014 book, *Hard Choices*, hits the market, her prose is, tellingly, critiqued from both the Right and Left for being too careful, too measured (Valenti 2014). This comes on the heels of her 2014 Benghazi testimony as secretary of state, when her heated exchange with Republican Ron Johnson served as fodder for this January 24 *New York Post* headline: "No Wonder Bill's Afraid: Hillary Explodes with Rage at Benghazi Hearing."[4] For Clinton, an emotional display—even in the form of a sharp retort—is read as a revelation of her "true state," which in turn renders her unfit for public office (angry, irrational, out of control). At the same time, her more typical careful, deliberate public persona is presented as a mere cover for her political motivations. As Jessica Valenti writes in her *Guardian* column, "Whenever she's hinted at being anything other than

measured and guarded, Clinton has been attacked as hysteri-
cal, a ballbuster or worse" (Valenti 2014). And while her book
is now criticized for being calculated and boring—not revealing enough of the emotional heat the public both chastises and
craves—the discussion remains focused on blaming Clinton as
an individual rather than on how limited is the range of culturally acceptable emotions for women in public office. For
Clinton, both displaying and not displaying emotion can be per-
ilous—and the pressing question is why this is so.

If we examine, as part of the rhetorical analyses we engage
with students, how emotion becomes part of public rhetoric,
we can begin to tease out some of the ways emotions are culturally interpreted, schooled, and disciplined. For instance,
in examining Obama's anger in the Wall Street case versus
Clinton's tears, it became evident that many viewers perceived
Obama as separate from his emotions. He is assumed to use
emotion—pathos—to procure a particular rhetorical effect. In
this way, he performs as an "emotionally intelligent" subject,
deploying his anger as a rationally chosen strategy to reach his
audience. While there was also some speculation that Clinton's
tears were contrived, they were read by some, in any case, as
having helped her secure a victory in New Hampshire because
they assured voters of her "humanness." They were interpreted, that is, as something *within* her that she finally allowed
to surface. The difference, then, is this: Clinton *has* emotions
and Obama *uses* emotions.

Studying the Clinton moment also helped us to begin to consider the strong emotional response that the emotions of subordinate groups can evoke in dominant groups, which moved
us a step closer to examining our own emotional responses to
texts as part of our pedagogical histories, something I explore
in the next section.

EMOTIONAL RESPONSES AS/TO TEXTS

If we are schooled at the site of emotions, such that our felt
responses are not simply natural or private but learned and

social, then our emotioned responses to texts become a legitimate part of classroom inquiry. This seems particularly important when an emotional response serves to stymie intellectual engagement, as in, "This is just how I feel," or, alternatively, when the writer is deemed too emotional and thereby dismissed. When teaching texts by writers from marginalized groups, for instance, I often confront student readings that dismiss the text by diagnosing the *writer* as "whiny," "angry," or "emotional." The problem is twofold. First, the reader moves away from a consideration of the text itself, which shuts down possibilities for analyzing rhetorical strategies and choices. Second, the reader equates the text with the writer and ultimately deems the text not worth engaging because of the writer's presumed emotional state. That is, if the writer is perceived as less than a rational subject, she is thereby muted.

My typical strategy of response in moments like this is to shift our focus back to the text and to its rhetorical contexts. While this is usually somewhat effective, its drawback is that it does not necessarily invite readers to account for their own emotional response to the text. It does not, as Boler puts it, allow us to "explore the revealed 'space' between ideology and internalized feeling" (Boler 1999, 13).

Although this was not my pedagogical intention, a moment during a Rhetoric of Women Writers course opened possibilities for us to employ this kind of exploration Boler promotes. That semester the Rhetoric of Women Writers was a 400/800-level course, enrolling both advanced undergraduate and graduate students. The course examines women's discursive practices and their relationship to the 2,000-year tradition of rhetoric, considering how women's contributions have subverted and transformed traditional assumptions about rhetorical theory and practice.

During the week our class focused on female silence, we discussed Gloria Anzaldúa's piece "How to Tame a Wild Tongue." Annie, a senior, led us to engage a passage from *Borderlands* that wasn't part of our assigned reading but that she had read in another class. Since she readily embraced most of Anzaldúa's ideas, her emotional discomfort with and resistance to the piece disturbed and preoccupied her. She read this passage to the group:

> Individually, but also as a racial entity, we [Chicano/as] need to voice our needs. We need to say to white society: We need you to accept the fact that Chicanos are different, to acknowledge your rejection and negation of us. We need you to own the fact that you looked upon us as less than human, that you stole our lands, our personhood, our self-respect. We need you to make public restitution: to say that, to compensate for your own sense of defectiveness, you strive for power over us, you erase our history and our experience because it makes you feel guilty—you'd rather forget your brutish acts. (Anzaldúa 1987, 85–86)

Several students spoke up to suggest that Annie was not wrong to feel offended by Anzaldúa's prose in this passage. "It's too angry to be useful," one student said. Another remarked that Anzaldúa simply "puts readers off" with these kinds of accusations, further dividing racial groups. One student labeled the passage a "rant." In our discussion of Anzaldúa's list of demands, I took my usual tack of articulating them as a rhetorical strategy rather than a spontaneous "rant." "Why might Anzaldúa have chosen to rely on such evocative language?" I asked. Some other students joined in with their own questions. "Who is her audience?" and "Can't it be useful to evoke discomfort and anger in her readers?" While these questions are good ones, in retrospect, I can see that my efforts aimed to establish Anzaldúa's emotion as a *rational* choice, to show that she was using anger in a calculated manner, as in the reading of Obama offered above. The risk of this strategy is that it might undercut the anger itself by containing it as a mere rhetorical tool. Instead, I could have asked, "Can one not be logical and angry at the same time?" Or "How is her anger a rational response?"

As our discussion ensued, I did point out to Annie that Anzaldúa issues similarly charged demands to Chicano men, which presumably didn't evoke this kind of emotional response in Annie. "Why not?" I asked. Annie explained that she responded defensively to the charge against white people, and not to the equally impassioned directives toward Chicano men, because she felt blamed for a historical situation in which she played no part. Consequently, she met Anzaldúa's anger with anger of her own and didn't know what to do with that response. To her credit, she made this felt tension a site of inquiry. That is, she sought to understand the space between her feeling and the ideology and assumptions that inform it.

In response to Annie, Marc, a student who had never before spoken in class, raised his hand to describe his life in a small Nebraska town, where he was raised by his white father and Puerto Rican mother. In this town, he said, where white people significantly outnumbered people of color, there existed a great deal of both "brown pride" and "brown anger." "But the anger isn't directed at any one individual," he insisted. "You shouldn't feel offended by the anger of minority people. We're mad at the system; we're not mad at any one white person. And we need that anger. It can feel really good and empowering." Marc's response to Annie was important in that it called attention to anger as an emotion that means and is experienced differently depending on the particular subject and the social contexts at play. Marc understood anger as a (logical) response to injustice, an emotion that bolsters a group's sense of righteous indignation. As I note above, to feel anger is to assume the position of judge and, in the case of "brown anger," to claim an emotion and position long denied to this group of people.

But there is another kind of anger, the anger expressed at Anzaldúa's seeming audacity to judge dominant groups. Boler describes this as "defensive anger," an anger not accounted for within Aristotle's definition or within "emotional intelligence." This breed of anger, she suggests, is a protective emotion that stems from a need to defend "one's investments in the values of the dominant culture" (Boler 1999, 191). Boler contends that two key features undergird defensive anger: "fear as a response to change, and a fear of loss" (192). The loss might involve a sense of privilege or even identity. For instance, Annie shared that her discomfort with Anzaldúa's passage led her to question her identity as a feminist and as a leftist thinker. Rather than aiming to manage or "shake off" the emotion, she treated it as a source for inquiry.

While there is not a simple litmus test to distinguish between moral and defensive anger—for either the person experiencing the feeling or for an outsider—the difference is still worth exploring, since both kinds of anger can be useful resources for inquiry. As Audre Lorde writes, "My anger is a response to racist attitudes and to the actions and presumptions that arise out of those attitudes. If your dealings with other women reflect those attitudes, then my anger and your attendant fears are spotlights that can be used for growth" (Lorde 1984, 124). Rather than deemed a "negative" emotion, then, anger is repurposed as a pathway for change.

This inquiry into and out of emotion cannot occur, however, unless emotion is understood as one feature of meaning making equal to other features and thereby deserving of a legitimate role in pedagogical settings. Just as writing and rhetoric teachers help students develop strategies to read with rhetorical contexts and strategies in mind, we might also work with students to develop a vocabulary for a rhetoric of emotion. This would involve helping students to rethink normative conceptions of emotion, in and outside of the academy, so as to establish that emotional responses are part and parcel of our intellectual work; grappling with new ideas will necessarily both employ and evoke emotion. Indeed, emotion can either serve as a powerful reinforcement of one's current beliefs or it can become, as Lorde suggests, a signal that one should reflect and investigate the sources of one's emotions.

The issue, then, is not whether emotion is a part of rhetorical inquiry—it undoubtedly is—but what we *do* with emotions. To relegate emotional response outside the classroom is to naturalize it, to assume its distinction from knowledge making. But to make it visible and emphasize its connections to personal histories, cultural norms and values, and institutional expectations is to open a new avenue for critical, reflective work; it is to repurpose emotion. A pedagogy that values emotion as a resource considers how our emotional investments determine what we choose to see and not see, listen and not listen to, accept or reject. It requires deliberate attention to how we have developed particular emotional investments over our life histories and how these investments subsequently shape subjectivity and color the lenses through which we view the world.

Annie's discussion of her discomfort both with Anzaldúa's text and her emotional response to it helped us to collectively consider how we might use emotions like guilt, fear, or anger as a starting point for dialogue, rather than as "bricks in a wall against which we all flounder" (Lorde 1984, 124). While Marc's remark reminded us that racially charged anger may not be targeted at individual subjects, the conversation led us to think about what it means to move from defensive anger to what Krista Ratcliffe calls a "responsibility logic," which requires us to account for the "historically situated discourses" that shape our listening and our positions as listeners (Ratcliffe 1999, 208). This includes a consideration of how all of us are "culturally implicated in the effects of the past" even if we are not responsible for the origins of the problem (Ratcliffe 2005, 32). This raised new questions for our class: What emotional responses prevent or enable my listening to a particular text or voice? What does it mean to live, at least momentarily, with painful or uncomfortable feelings that emerge when we understand that systems that violate others benefit us? What does it mean to be responsible to, rather than guilty for, these situations?

Repurposing emotion as a resource means making such questions a regular part of students' engagement with course texts and one another's contributions. But it would also make emotional inquiry a regular component of rhetorical analysis—along with considerations of historical moment, context, audience, purpose, ethos, and so on—to investigate how the writer/speaker used emotion as a site of knowledge production. Students might also be asked to consider what emotions the course readings evoked and, importantly, to follow this by accounting for the ways the social sphere shapes these responses. The task, then, would be to make a reflection on that "revealed 'space' between ideology and internalized feeling" a regular part of the pedagogy (Boler 1999, 13).

NEW PURPOSES, NEW POSSIBILITIES OF EMOTION

Feminist repurposing involves disrupting normative repetitions in order to investigate the social contexts that give rise to them. But it also involves discovery of new possibility; this often occurs as a result of embracing what has been cast off, suppressed, or quarantined. From this "waste," feminists discover new possibilities for agency and (re)invention. This is particularly vital, since women have not historically had access to the same rhetorical opportunities or "available means of persuasion" as men—so they must invent their own. As Ritchie and Ronald point out, rhetorical invention for women often begins with locating a way to speak "in the context of being silenced and rendered invisible as persons" (Ritchie and Ronald 2001, xvii). Last semester, as my students and I studied the rhetoric of women writers from classical times to the contemporary moment, we noted the repetition of women navigating shame on their way to writing with agency. Shame, as Nancy Mairs writes, is the wrongness or insufficiency of one's very being. "I feel guilt or embarrassment for something I've done; shame, for who I am. I may stop doing bad or stupid things, but I can't stop being." (Mairs 2001, 397). And while the effect of shame is the cracking and stifling of her voice, Mairs discovers that "speaking out loud" is the "antidote to shame" (2001, 397). She moves, then, from being paralyzed in shame to writing from and revealing shame, through the cracks and despite the stifling. In so doing, she repurposes shame from a debilitating emotion to the impetus for cultural critique and self-representation.

I call attention to feminist repurposing of shame because it is understood not only as a destructive emotion but also as a feminine one. Aristotle names shame as "womanish" and Freud as a "feminine characteristic par excellence" (quoted in Locke 2007, 148). Moreover, because it is embodied—accompanied by a visceral blush—it is often relegated to the private, to the realm of the unspeakable. But feminist writers show that writing shame illuminates the scripts that trigger shaming (Locke 2007; Probyn 2005). Repurposing shame—as with all emotional inquiry—requires severing its strict tie to the individual to instead approach it as a catalyst to investigate the social conditions that give rise to it. One of our course texts, Nomy Lamm's "It's a Big Fat Revolution" helps demonstrate this. Lamm describes a TV ad that depicts a "teary-eyed fat girl who says, 'I've tried everything, but nothing works. I lost twenty pounds, and I gain back twenty-five. I feel so ashamed. What can I do?'" (Lamm 2001, 458). Lamm cries in response to the ad. She writes, "I know that feeling of shame . . . But I know that the unhappiness is not a result of my fat. It's a result of a society that tells me I'm bad" (458). She then launches a critique of a culture that deems weight discrimination acceptable and conflates fatness with lack of willpower. For Lamm, shame is mined to excavate and reveal toxic cultural values and to speak from an embodied position often rendered invisible and degraded.

Mairs also repurposes shame by writing the connection between her disabled body and her voice. She lets us see her husband carry her to the emergency room after a suicide attempt, "my hair matted, my face swollen and gray, my nightgown streaked with blood and urine . . . I was a body, and one in a hell of a mess. I should have kept quiet about that experience. I know the rules of polite discourse" (Mairs 2001, 398). Part of departing from her shame, though, means dislodging the boundaries around politeness. As Probyn writes, "It's not that the effects of shame can be harnessed by stories; it's that shame demands that we tell other stories" (Probyn 2005, 72). Shame repurposed, then, opens avenues for new cultural narratives.

One of my students, in fact, enacted this disruption and revision in her engagement with Mairs's story. Alison, then a second-year doctoral student, wrote that her response to Mairs's piece was visceral—uneasy, a little embarrassed. Mairs broke the conventions of polite discourse, which would have required her to hush the story of her suicide attempt. Or to narrate it without reminding us of the blood, the urine, the mess, the shame—to get on top of it, control it. In responding to the text, Alison had to make a decision, too. Alison writes:

> I was surprised by the discomfort I felt as Mairs discusses the connections between her body and voice . . . I was surprised by her honesty, her embodied prose. I couldn't help but consider how Mairs' words, her voice and persona, differed from the (disembodied) writing style I was used to reading and writing in academia.
>
> My process of composing a response to Mairs' piece was discomforting, even painful. And it came in pieces. As I wrote, I was all too aware of the sense that "'full, excessive lives' push against the 'strict limits of texts that must be ironed out, made unwrinkled and smooth'" (Welch qtd in Jung 40). I was aware of my desire to make the text neat—to leave out details, to remove narratives that didn't seem "academic" enough. (Friedow 2009, 13)

The pain and discomfort Alison experienced as she engaged Mairs's text led her to examine the contours of her own academic writing. Until this point, she used her reading responses to explore potential dissertation topics, following, as she put it, a regular pattern of response in which she "briefly summarize[d] the piece, analyze[d] the main points, pose[d] a few questions" (Friedow 2009, 14). This pattern also allowed her a comfortable distance from the text, a distance that Mairs's piece seemed to refuse.

Ultimately, Alison took a risk and wrote a piece that diverged from her previous work, but one that felt, at least to me, far more powerful. She wove theories of embodiment and language with stories of her own emotional history of learning to associate her body with shame, embarrassment, and anxiety:

> As I think about my own history as an embodied woman, I'm reminded of the shame I was taught to associate with my own body. There was great anxiety in my house around bodies. For example, my mother would come into my room at night to be sure the blinds were closed as we changed into our pajamas. When we came down the stairs in the morning, she would wait at the bottom to okay my choice of dress before allowing me to go to school; bodies had to be properly contained and covered. To this day, I see her worried gaze as I look in the mirror and analyze my reflection.

When I shared with Alison that her voice sounded stronger, clearer, in this text, even as she felt less certain, she replied,

"I just couldn't write in the same academic way in response to this piece. It called for a different kind of voice." Here Alison experienced in her own writing what so many of the writers we read over the semester also articulated: feminist purposes—and repurposing—often call for new forms, new enactments that require working with uncertainty. As we e-mailed about her piece, Alison explained her process this way: "There were several times as I was writing it that I stopped and just decided I would write a more traditional response, but when I tried to do that, it just didn't feel genuine, it just felt like writing in a way that didn't matter to me, and I kept going back to writing about my visceral reactions to Mairs' essay."

I'm struck that Alison refers to her feelings of both dissonance and connection with the text as the primary catalyst for this new mode of response and the subject of discussion in her work. This is exactly how Jaggar imagines outlaw emotions to function: "The new emotions evoked by feminist insights are likely in turn to stimulate further feminist observations and insights, and these may generate new directions in both theory and political practice. There is a continuous feedback loop between our emotional constitution and our theorizing such that each continually modifies the other and is in principle inseparable from it" (Jaggar 1989, 147).

If emotion is, in fact, deemed inseparable from theory making, then we might encourage our students not to divorce a felt response from their intellectual work but to use it as a resource for further investigation. While doing so is neither efficient nor pain-free, as Alison's reflection suggests, it refuses to mask emotion as a "dominant cultural category" (Worsham 1998, 224), and it insists that emotion is integral, not ancillary, to both the development of new knowledge and the inclusion of new voices. For Alison, the new knowledge constituted not only a deepened understanding of the ties between her own embodiment, gender, and voice, but also extended her thinking about the constraints and possibilities of traditional academic writing.

When I asked Alison how the pedagogy of the course might have enabled her inquiry, Alison noted that a "low-stakes" writing space established as a dialogue among the student, the text, and me, the teacher, was important to this mode of exploration. She added, however, "But then I guess the question is how do we invite students to actually take up the opportunity we offer?" since, as she pointed out, "I didn't use the writing space this way until I felt confronted by something I just could not ignore, but when that happened, the opportunity/space for writing and engaging this knowledge was there." As Alison's experience demonstrates, students can't be forced to engage in a different kind of knowledge making; however, if an invitation is issued, and if that invitation is reinforced by textual models in the course readings, then, as she suggests, the space is there should students wish to occupy it.

Alison indicates other conditions that contributed to her willingness to engage in this kind of writing: "The framing of rhetorical listening early in our class, my knowledge of your areas of scholarly interest, and the topic of the course may have all influenced my willingness and desire to explore this connection." But perhaps most significant, Alison underscores the importance of teacher response to alternative forms and paths of knowledge making:

> One question I've been struggling to answer . . . is what I would have done had you not responded in the way you did to my paper. What might have happened if I felt reprimanded in some way (or even just simply ignored) rather than encouraged to explore this connection further? I probably would not have continued to theorize from this experience; I may not have written the [eventual] essay [for publication]; I may have been afraid to explore further inquiry into embodied teaching and learning; so, pedagogically, there are acts of sponsorship throughout the trajectory of the course. It seems that your response to my risk fueled my inquiry and furthered my process of (public) knowledge-making with emotion.

Pedagogies that embrace rather than excise emotion not only help students to understand emotion as part of reading and composing but also help them to consider what there is to learn from that which our culture would throw out. In fact, attending to a rhetoric of emotion in both published texts and the texts of our lives helps us to see emotion as fertile ground for new purposes, new possibilities.

THE RHETORIC OF EMOTION

While the recent heightened attention to emotional intelligence presents an opportunity to rethink the role of emotion in educational processes, it also highlights the need to examine the normative conceptions of emotion that inform it. To return to the example mentioned at the outset of this chapter, for instance, Morga (2011) credits organizations like the Collaborative for Academic, Social and Emotional Learning (n.d.) (CASEL) as a step in the right direction, but she argues that there are not yet enough efforts to educate the public and to address the "stigma attached to emotions." A look at the factors listed as evidence of CASEL's success helps illuminate why this stigma remains: significant improvement of standardized tests scores, less disruptive classroom behavior, and decreased need for discipline (CASEL FAQs). CASEL's success, then, is determined largely by neoliberal measures of individual success and self-control. Until emotions are repurposed as a resource, rather than deemed as renegade or irrational and therefore in need of management, the "stigma attached to emotions" is not likely to dissipate.

Alternatively, feminist repurposing of emotion illuminates the normative view of emotion and seeks to enact it differently—as a resource for new ways of knowing, reading, and being in the world. Earlier in this chapter, I referenced Brené Brown's vulnerability and shame research, first featured in a TEDTalk that has garnered almost 9 million hits and later promoted by Oprah and in other national media outlets. She's a striking example of someone who has repurposed emotions deemed deeply negative as an integral part of courage and creativity—but not without some public recoiling.

In her second TEDTalk, Brown indicates that the success of her initial talk led to requests for her to speak but the invitations, she notes, were often presented with conditions that aimed to omit the very emotions that occupy the center of her work:

> After the TED explosion, I got a lot of offers to speak all over the country—everyone from schools and parent meetings to Fortune 500 companies. And so many of the calls went like this, "Hey, Dr. Brown. We loved your TEDTalk. We'd like you to come in and speak. We'd appreciate it if you wouldn't mention vulnerability or shame." What would you like for me to talk about? There's three big answers. This is mostly, to be honest with you, from the business sector: innovation, creativity and change. (Brown 2012)

These businesses wanted Brown to inspire the seeming ingredients of success in a way that excluded her key research subjects—shame and vulnerability—from the mix. Brown's response, though, is to argue that these emotions are all of a piece; they cannot be separated: "So let me go on the record and say, vulnerability is the birthplace of innovation, creativity and change. To create is to make something that has never existed before. There's nothing more vulnerable than that. Adaptability to change is all about vulnerability" (Brown 2012).

While feminists and the business sector may seek different outcomes, enabling students to innovate, create, and change has the potential to serve both civic life and the economy. These are traits, however, that require more than skills or the ability to "manage" emotions or behave according to society's norms; they require the engagement of emotions as a resource, as part of the recipe of creating something new. Feminist repurposing moves us away from viewing emotion as a problem to be controlled and managed, instead offering a new kind of emotional discourse, one that engages, inquires, and mines emotion as a resource for new ways of knowing, writing, and being. When emotion is regarded as epistemic, it no longer falls outside of rationalism; indeed, I contend that rational inquiry requires us to consider emotion as part of knowledge making.

In the next chapter, I move to another "feminine" sphere

appropriated by neoliberal discourse as a marketable skill: listening. As with emotion, I argue that feminist perspectives are vital to conceptions of listening, in order to prompt richer conceptions of dialogue.

NOTES

1. The concept of emotional intelligence was picked up by Oprah Winfrey and *Time* magazine and covered on National Public Radio. Goleman (1995) has followed his original text with companion volumes (2000, 2004, 2007, 2008) and an updated anniversary edition (2006).

2. In the tradition of feminist scholars like Jaggar, Boler, and Micciche, I use the term *emotion* rather than *affect, feeling*, or *passion* because it is the word most commonly relied upon in dominant discourse (in particular, as I will discuss below, with regard to "emotional intelligence"), and thus is most in need of denaturalization and revision.

3. See, for instance, Quandahl's (2003) "A Feeling for Aristotle," in which she argues for Aristotle as a crucial predecessor for arguments about emotion as integral to rhetorical work.

4. When Senator Johnson pressed Clinton on whether she could have immediately determined the motive of the Benghazi attack, she snapped, "With all due respect, the fact is we had four dead Americans. Was it because of a protest? Or was it because of guys out for a walk one night who decided they'd go kill some Americans? What difference, at this point, does it make?" (CSPAN 2013).

3

REPURPOSING LISTENING
From Agonistic to Rhetorical

In a feature on *NPR Marketplace*, reporter Bill Radke spotlights a rising trend in improving business for health insurance companies: empathy training. Because of health-care reform and industry competition, insurance companies have reason to be concerned about customer retention—especially when consumer research shows that customers don't feel their insurance company cares about them or their health. The solution? Better customer "care," which includes feeling heard, understood, and empathized with. Radke gives the audience a chance to eavesdrop on this training, in which customer service representatives are taught to make empathetic statements, to offer a "successful" apology, and to "smile with their voice." All in the name of customer loyalty. Not to put too fine a point on it, Radke says, "The next time you call customer service and you hear, 'I care, I understand. I understand your frustration regarding this issue' or 'I hear what you're saying,' . . . that's the sound of an agent trying not to get fired" (quoted in Warner 2010).

Indeed, listening is big business. As early as 1952, *Harvard Business Review* named listening a highly desirable workplace skill, and attention to listening in private industry—how it is defined, what it enables, how it can be studied, and how it can be taught—only continues to grow. In fact, in their article "Listening in the Business Context," Jan Flynn, Tuula-Riitta Valikoski, and Jennie Grau claim that "listening is proposed to be the most valued interpersonal skill necessary for success in numerous fields" (Flynn, Valikoski, and Grau 2008, 144). The purported benefits of "listening efficiency" are abundant: it helps one get hired; determines promotion; increases sales performance; and enhances perceptions of trustworthiness,

DOI: 10.7330/9781607323884.c003

motivation, and production (Flynn, Valikoski, and Grau 2008; Janusik 2002). To capitalize on these benefits, it is now regular practice for corporations to offer "listening training," which emphasizes skills like interpreting and providing verbal and nonverbal cues, paraphrasing, reflecting, and asking questions (Janusik 2002, 23).

Listening has also been identified as a crucial skill for academic success. Studies indicate that college students who perform higher on listening tests—demonstrating focused attention, understanding, and retention—are also more likely to succeed academically, specifically in terms of grades (Beall et al. 2008, 126). Improved listening is also associated with reduced "wasted classroom time" and subsequently, more efficient learning (Beall et al. 2008, 124). At the K–12 level, listening skills are part of English language arts standards in thirty-eight states, which means listening, in those states, is now a skill for which students (and teachers) are held accountable by the No Child Left Behind Act and, more recently, the Common Core Standards. Here listening is typically understood as comprehension of oral material in the classroom, with evidence of good listening associated with memory and attention (Beall et al. 2008; Janusik 2002). Despite agreement on the importance of listening, however, listening scholars in communications and rhetoric lament the dearth of research on listening instruction and call for greater attention to how listening is defined, taught, and measured (Imhof 1998, 2001; Janusik 2002).

While composition and rhetoric has not historically devoted significant attention to listening—Krista Ratcliffe (1999) names it as the neglected rhetorical trope—over the last decade scholars within feminist rhetoric have produced a rich body of work that aims to reclaim listening as part of the rhetorical tradition (Ballif and Mountford 2000; Jung 2005). Their conception of listening, however, diverges in some important ways from those calls made by business and K–12 education policymakers. Perhaps most notably, Ratcliffe's articulation of rhetorical listening establishes listening as a trope for interpretive invention and a means to facilitate cross-cultural dialogue (1999, 196).

Rhetorical listening disrupts what Ratcliffe calls "the organizing principle" of both disciplinary and cultural biases: a diminished notion of logos. While the Greek conception of logos included both listening and speaking—one dependent upon and equal to the other—the West inherited a divided logos that privileges speech at the expense of listening. By contrast, rhetorical listening stems from a restored logos, whose purpose is not to improve the prospects for the individual success of the hearer but instead to alter the dynamics of argument and dialogue in a way that emphasizes reflection, responsibility, and understanding of difference.

In what follows, I draw from feminist approaches to listening to repurpose its normative uses and enactments. I contend that while there is promise in increased public attention to listening, it still functions to serve neoliberal aims of profit and individual success. This normative mode of listening is not limited to corporate settings, however; I also show how our listening within the academy is shaped by logics that value competition and winning over dialogue and learning. I then draw from feminist articulations of a repurposed listening that rely upon a restored logos in order to articulate a pedagogy that makes rhetorical listening integral to argument. I show how repurposed listening can enhance how we understand our own positions and the perspectives of others and, in so doing, facilitate new possibilities for argumentation.

LISTENING FOR SUCCESS

As Ratcliffe points out, popular culture tends to naturalize listening as something we all do but no one needs to study. One reason for the low status listening occupies, she further contends, is its association with the "feminine"; that is, historically, listening serves as the passive counterpart to speech, signifying deference, support, or attentiveness. Drawing upon Deborah Tannen's study of listening and gender, Ratcliffe summarizes: "Men are socialized to play the listening game via the questions 'Have I won?' and 'Do you respect me?' while women are socialized to play it via the questions 'Have I been helpful?' and 'Do you like me?'" (Ratcliffe 1999, 200). Listening as deference is also evident if we consider who has been historically positioned as listener—so as to follow orders or to discern how to "fit in" to dominant culture—and who has occupied the position of speaker.

Neoliberal attention to listening, however, appropriates these "feminine" traits to its own ends. Both mainstream business articles and scholarly research (located mainly in communications) offer solid agreement about the importance of listening. Corporate leaders emphasize that listening is key to "fact-finding" and "intelligence-gathering from clients, customers, stakeholders, and the employees who are on the front lines of the marketplace" (Burnison 2010, 2). Listening is promoted as a means to assess consumer desires and market trends as well as a way to gauge consumer and employee satisfaction.

Within neoliberal discourse, the act of listening to one's subordinates is recast as a characteristic of strong leadership. For instance, on the website businesslistening.com, management trainer Madelyn Burley-Allen lists the benefits of workplace listening, including the "bond of respect" it creates between supervisor and employee. She writes, "Employees like, and respond better to, supervisors who they think are listening to them." In other words, listening is established as a strategy for presumably leveling the playing field, for behaving as equals, without actually altering the structural hierarchy. In a study of 122 supervisors across management levels, Husband et al. found that supervisors who listen well both gain more accurate information about business operations and create a "supportive interpersonal environment for the subordinate" (cited in Flynn, Valikoski, and Grau 2008, 144). Being heard gives the subordinate the feeling of a more collegial atmosphere, which in turn improves the business environment and workplace productivity.

Supervisory listening not only creates a better work environment for the employees, however; it is also a skill associated with career success and promotion. Indeed, studies indicate a connection between managerial listening and career achievement, given that upper-level management requires greater reliance on listening (Brownell 1994; Kotter 1982). So even while dominant cultural values privilege speech and persuasion over listening, research findings show that middle managers are likely to spend more time writing reports and engaging in efforts to persuade, while senior managers spend more time listening (Brownell 1994).

Just as emotion has been recast to promote individual success in the emotional intelligence movement, so, too, is listening appropriated as a deployable skill that can serve corporate outcomes and promote individual gains. Not surprisingly, then, listening training in the workplace is a booming industry. A look at the approaches that dominate this instruction further illuminates the values that animate this movement.

While recent listening theory emphasizes the dynamic, contextual nature of listening (Imhof 1998, 2001; Janusik 2002), most approaches to the study and improvement of listening rely on one of two models: cognitive or behavioral. Cognitive methods focus on the mental processes involved in listening, such as selecting, segregating, and integrating information (Imhof 1998, 82), while behavioral models attend to the observable interactions between speaker and listener. Janusik notes that because the cognitive processing involved in listening cannot be seen, we often perceive listening as behavioral—something that is demonstrated via observable performance like nodding or restating another's ideas—and therefore aim to improve listening by refining behaviors associated with listening. For instance, the company the Par Group's "Secrets to Listening Well" include the following: "Give 100 percent attention; respond verbally or nonverbally; prove understanding by occasionally restating the other person's idea or by asking a relevant question; and be respectful by demonstrating that you take other views seriously" (quoted in Reese 2009).

The skills-based approaches to listening found in corporate settings are also predominant in school settings—that is, when listening is taught at all. According to Beall et al., "Few schools offer listening instruction, and even in courses where listening is supposedly emphasized, only 7% of the time is devoted to listening" (2008, 123). When listening is addressed in postsecondary education, it is usually through a skills-based component of a communications class, even as listening is employed in all college classrooms. For instance, in their survey of communication textbooks with chapters devoted to listening, Janusik and Wolvin found that the treatment of listening was often "atheoretical," focused on "tips and techniques, and 'recipes' for how to listen" (quoted in Janusik 2002, 21). While listening was explained as a process in these texts, the approaches suggested to improve it were similar to corporate methods—identifying listening barriers and developing strategies (paraphrasing, reflecting, recognizing nonverbal cues, and so on) to overcome them.

Listening scholars Janusik and Imhof argue that these models come up short because they do not address the interplay of cognitive and behavioral components that listening requires or explore the contextual nature of listening, which involves attention to the "communication relationship" between speaker and listener (Janusik 2002, 26). Imhof further notes that prior knowledge, attitudes, and motivation for listening affect one's ability to listen—considerations that exceed what is addressed in skills-based approaches (Imhof 1998, 86). Indeed, in a study she conducted of university students in Germany, Imhof found that students struggled to listen "when they were not interested, when they felt that the subject was getting difficult, or when they did not agree with what was being said" (89). Of course, many of us might argue that these are exactly the moments when listening could most serve a student's learning, moving him or her out of entrenched positions to explore new ideas.

But within neoliberal approaches, what's important is not that genuine listening or dialogue is taking place; it is that employees or customers *perceive* that they are being heard. Recall Burley-Allen's aforementioned quotation: "Employees like, and respond better to, supervisors who they think are listening to them." While such behavioral methods might well sharpen verbal and nonverbal cues associated with listening, they do not promote listening to evoke change on the part of the listener, or encourage the supervisor to learn from, or think with, the employee. Nor do they allow for inquiry into the rhetorical contexts and social dynamics that enable or prevent listening. Listening is a means to information, smoother relationships between supervisors and employees, and greater productivity; its purpose is fine-tuning an existing structure, not revising its logics or values.

FEMINIST RHETORICAL LISTENING: A RESTORED LOGOS

While neoliberal conceptions of listening aim to improve operations within existing structures and relationships, repurposed listening attends to the dominant cultural codes and logics at play within discursive relationships. This work begins with illuminating our conceptions of logos, which function as what Ratcliffe calls "the organizing principle" of disciplinary and cultural biases toward listening (Ratcliffe 1999, 202).

According to Martin Heidegger, the West inherited *logos* as the Greek noun, understood as a system of reasoning and forming logic, but lost its verb form, *legein,* which means not only to speak but also "to lay down, to lay before"—that is, to listen (1975, 60). The result is an impoverished notion of language that relies on an "arrogant" logos, which excludes particular voices and perpetuates a homogenized mode of speech based on competition rather than dialogue (Fiumara 1995, 6). Or, as Wayne Booth puts it, the result is a rhetoric that overvalues the question "How can I change your mind?" and undervalues "When should I change my mind?" (Booth 2005, 379). We need, of course, only turn on CNN to see evidence of a culture that views argument as a game to be won, where listening functions like playing defense—guarding one's position while the opponent has the microphone.

Feminists scholars, however, repurpose listening as an active, generative practice that allows us to hear beyond our entrenched positions and assumptions. Here, speech and listening are reciprocal practices that, together, sponsor the creation of new knowledge. When listening is rhetorical, it is conceived as more than a set of behaviors, an aural perception, or a cognitive function: it involves all of these processes, which are shaped by social contexts and cultural logics, and which, like writing, require investigation, practice, and reflection.

First, and perhaps foremost, to listen rhetorically requires "a capacity and willingness" to situate oneself openly in relation to discourse, whether written, spoken, or imagistic (Ratcliffe 1999, 204; Rayner 1993). That is, one must be willing—indeed, to view it as a responsibility—to listen with the purpose of movement beyond one's established knowledge and positions. This involves an awareness of what we bring, as listeners, to the exchange. As Ratcliffe observes, we listen not just for the speaker/writer's intent but with our own "self-interested intent," which is often so naturalized that it escapes conscious awareness (Ratcliffe 1999, 205). This "intent" is related to the multiple and fluid locations from which we hear, and which result in fluctuating degrees of openness to listening. As Rayner writes, "The individual hears with varying capacities, from varying positions, from differing interests, from one moment to the next" (Rayner 1993, 4). By articulating the locations and interests from which we listen—as a mother, a student, a Democrat, a lesbian, a Muslim, an administrator, and so on—we may become more conscious of how we interact with what we hear, which, in turn, may helps us expand our capacities to listen.

Rhetorical listening also requires explicit attention to the relationship between speaker and listener. What are the power dynamics between us? What are our (presumed) commonalities and differences? What cultural logics, values, and assumptions shape the position of the speaker (Ratcliffe 1999, 204)? Here, listening is indeed an act of interpretive invention (Ratcliffe 1999) because it involves both inquiring into and imagining the histories and logics that shape another's claims. And doing so nudges us away from easy dismissal of another's ideas. Instead, we must ask: How and why might the speaker have arrived at this claim? What cultural histories might have shaped this position? And, ultimately, how does attending to these cultural logics help us discover new capacities to listen, or to consider our differences?

These questions are vital if the goal of listening is enhanced dialogue and understanding across difference. That is, attention to implicit context, logics, and histories help sponsor listening when, as Rayner suggests, hearing is not "automatic" or easy, does not come out of "common culture, language, race or gender" or from a shared exigency (Rayner 1993, 6). For Ratcliffe, the practice of "standing under"—an inversion of understanding—is the purpose of rhetorical listening. Standing under our own discourses, she writes, means "identifying the various discourses embodied in each of us and then listening to hear and imagine how they might affect not only ourselves but others." Standing under the discourse of others means acknowledging the logics and histories that shape their claims, "listening for the (un)conscious presences, absences, and unknowns," and "consciously integrating this information into our worldviews and decision-making" (Ratcliffe 1999, 206). It requires, then, developing a more acute and expansive receptivity that allows us to consider what we cannot immediately hear. It requires time and space for dwelling and integrating.

In reading Ratcliffe's work for class, one of my advanced undergraduate students aptly responded, "But if we're so busy doing all of this analysis, we can't really be present to listen!" I couldn't disagree. But rhetorical listening, I would contend, expands beyond the act that occurs in the moment of exchange. Like a rich writing process, it requires time, reflection, and many returns to the text, as new ideas and perspectives arise. Fiumara describes listening in Western culture as more "involved in hunting than in cultivation" (1995, 10). Rhetorical listening aims to reverse that. Indeed, listening to cultivate means that there is always more to consider; at the same time, making rhetorical listening a habit of mind may also remind us to listen with openness in the moment of the exchange.

Feminist repurposing of listening, then, aims to engender "truer forms of dialogue" (Fiumara 1995, 13), greater understanding (and questioning) of the cultural logics that shape our own listening and others' speech, and increased possibilities for inventing, interpreting, and arguing. It helps us to move beyond a habitual listening-for-gain approach, which, as I'll show, is evident in academic as well as corporate sites, in order to allow for listening that hears a greater range of perspectives, including those voices most often drowned out or muted. Because rhetorical listening is rarely modeled or taught, I turn now to consider what it means to sponsor a repurposed listening in pedagogical sites, first showing how this breaks normative academic practice of engaging others' voices.

LISTENING TO OTHERS: BEYOND "THEY SAY, I SAY"

How do we listen, and teach our students to listen, to others within academic discourse? Gerald Graff and Cathy Birkenstein, in *They Say/I Say: The Moves that Matter in Academic Writing,* note that "the underlying structure of academic writing—and of responsible public discourse—resides not just in stating our own ideas but in listening closely to others around us" (Graff and Birkenstein 2006, 3). Chris Thaiss and Terry Myers Zawacki's 2006 cross-disciplinary study underscores a similar sentiment: faculty interviewed across disciplines emphasized the importance of a writer attending to and reflecting on the conversation he or she seeks to enter (Thaiss and Zawacki 2006, 5). In fact, they point out that faculty are "invariably harsh toward any student or scholar who hasn't done the background reading" (2006, 5). While we may teach students to start with what "they say" or to do the "background reading," however, the aims of such a practice are not necessarily the same as fostering an ability to *listen* to the scholarly dialogue they engage.

Within a neoliberal logic, attending to the words of others often serves as a way to pave the road for one's own contribution, not to engage in genuine dialogue with other scholars. In this way, then, predominant modes of listening in academia overlap with those in corporate models: both value listening as a means to an individually driven end. For instance, in their chapter "The Art of Summarizing," Graff and Birkenstein instruct that "a good summary . . . has a focus or spin that allows the summary to fit with your own overall agenda while still being true to the text you are summarizing (Graff and Birkenstein 2006, 31–32). The predetermined agenda of the writer drives listening, which necessarily determines *how* other voices are heard. As Ratcliffe points out, the traditional habit of academic reading is to discern "what we can agree with or challenge" (1999, 203). How, in other words, can I use this text to serve my project? Listening, then, becomes a way to ensure a solid defense while formulating a well-planned attack.

Rhetorical listening, alternatively, leaves room and space for engagement. It is, as Fiumara describes, "characterized by the requirement that we dwell with, abide by, whatever we try to know; that we aim at coexistence with, rather than knowledge-of" (Fiumara 1995, 16). Assuming a listening stance begins with an intention to consider, "How does this expand what I know?" or "What does this teach me about my own worldview or social location?" It is a practice aimed at opening possibilities across commonalities and differences rather than digging more deeply into entrenched positions.

But what does it mean to instruct student writers in such a practice? Recently, in teaching a 300-level course called Rhetoric: Argument and Society, I made it a course goal to unpack normative modes of argument with my students, considering what it would mean to enact a logos that places speech and listening in a reciprocal relationship. Since repurposing habitual practices requires illuminating the normative, we began by thinking together about the role of listening in our educational and family histories. How did you learn to listen? How do you know when someone is listening? Who, according to cultural norms, is typically expected to do the listening? What does it mean to listen?

Most students could not articulate specific moments of learning to listen, except by way of following the directions or orders of a parent or a teacher. Listening, they pointed out, is something we expect children, subordinates, and often women to do. When I played for them the NPR clip with which I open this chapter, a few of them who had worked telemarketing jobs could relate. They told stories of getting hung up on, sworn at, and treated disrespectfully—but nevertheless being required to remain polite and attentive. Listening, they discerned, is often equated with "service" work.

As we moved on to consider the role of listening in argument—watching clips of political debates and reading excerpts from Tannen's (1999) "Argument Culture," Lamb's 1991 "Beyond Argument in Feminist Composition," and Ratcliffe's 1999 "Rhetorical Listening"—the normative conceptions of speaking, listening, and arguing no longer seemed adequate. They seemed, as many students observed, more like fighting (to win) than arguing (to learn). While we could collectively point to numerous examples of learning to persuade or to hone one's message, from standardized writing tests to debate team to Facebook updates, it was more difficult to point to cultural examples of rhetorical listening. I asked them to pay attention in their daily lives to acts of listening and to see if they could find examples of listening rhetorically.

One of my students, a journalism major, pointed us to a Chinese news show called *Dialogue* as an alternate approach to the Western two-sided, point, counterpoint model. In class, we watched a short clip of a discussion on gun control in the United States. The show aired about a month after the Sandy Hook Elementary shooting, and the discussion included the moderator, the show's current affairs commentator, the former Chinese ambassador to Sweden, and an associate professor at the People's Public Security University of China. My students and I noted that, in contrast to U.S. cable news network shows, the guests did not talk over one another, raise their voices to create heightened drama, or make faces while their colleagues spoke. The pacing of conversation was slower and more deliberate, as each participant added layers to the dialogue that showed the complexity of the issues surrounding gun control—pointing, for instance, to the historical context in which the Second Amendment was ratified, the large number of U.S. households with guns, the divisive role of the NRA, and the function of background checks and automatic weapons. While my students rightly noted that these commentators had the luxury of distance—discussing U.S. culture, not their own—they were also struck by the performed willingness to fully flesh out the problem rather than speaking out of predetermined positions. They noted that this conversation broke the repetition of pro– or anti–Second Amendment stances they felt dominated cable news—or at least the sound bites that reverberate across media outlets in the United States.

While our engagement with this show was admittedly brief, it helped us to think about how we learn to listen (or not) in a culture that privileges cross-fire-type exchanges and that views winning as the desired outcome of argument. Perhaps most important, we thought about what it meant for us to listen to this dialogue, wherein we were not so much steered toward an answer or to a side as invited to place complex, historical, and cultural perspectives together. This listening, then, was more oriented toward dwelling with multiplicity than choosing one side of a duality. It also helped us consider how we listen and speak from multiple perspectives, which are not typically solid or uniform. For instance, during the clip, Einar Tangen, the current affairs commentator, points out that with 88 percent of U.S. citizens owning guns, there exists a range of perspectives among them about gun control measures—they are not all simply "gun nuts." In fact, he goes on to point out that this is not simply a party-line issue but rather a complex one fueled by history and fear. My students and I discussed, then, how seeing many facets to an issue allows greater opportunities for locating what Ratcliffe calls "discursive spaces of both commonalities and differences" (Ratcliffe 1999, 204). Here, both commonalities and differences are viewed as "possible metonymic places for rhetorical exchanges" (209), such that even where differences exist, there is space available for learning.

Part of teaching rhetorical listening—or repurposing listening in our classrooms—requires more opportunity to dwell in, or "abide by," the multiple facets and perspectives that shape the dialogue about a given issue. Since we are used to listening to agree or disagree, this requires deliberate practice, to which I turn in the next section.

LISTENING FOR MULTIPLICITY

In a culture that values efficient decisions and equates certainty with strength (we need only think about politicians who change their minds or consult others being dubbed "wafflers" or about timed standardized tests that demand a persuasive essay in thirty minutes), students are not often practiced at delaying judgment to make time for listening to complexity. As I've discussed above, we often learn to read for points of agreement or disagreement, without reflecting on the factors that shape our position in the first place. In her book *Revisionary Rhetoric, Feminist Pedagogy, and Multigenre Texts*, Julie Jung contends that promoting alternatives to monologic discourse requires us to develop strategies that encourage listening to a full range of voices, prompting a movement from dualistic thinking to multiplicity. I agree that students are in need of new processes and practices that help support rhetorical listening—and that break the repetition of reading to summarize or to dismiss. In both cases, the reader/listener might be viewed as consuming a text rather than participating in dialogue with it (Jung 2005, 34).

I began this process with my students—in the aforementioned Rhetoric: Argument and Society course—in their low-stakes weekly response writing. While I have often left such response writing open, I find that, understandably, in response to the blank page, students often either summarize the text to show comprehension, or they agree or disagree with the text, often based on the degree to which they find it relatable. Neither of these practices are inherently problematic, but they don't foster the practice of listening to multiple perspectives, including the students' own, that enables rhetorical listening. So, instead, I ask them to address two questions[1]:

1. How does this reading build on, complicate, or enrich what we've already learned about rhetoric and argument?

2. How does this reading connect to my daily life, to other texts
we've read, to arguments I've recently encountered, or that
I want to make myself?

With the first question, my aim is to help students put texts and
ideas together in dialogue and to consider how placing ideas
side by side, letting them dwell together, enhances (and often
complicates) our understanding of a concept like argument or
rhetoric. Sometimes students expect that texts in a syllabus will
lead them progressively to an "answer" or to the correct view
of an issue—such that each text represents a critique of the
one prior. Other times they may hold onto valorized texts—in
this case, Plato and Aristotle—as the ones that are perpetually
"correct" because of their cultural status. It takes time, then, to
help them come to understand that I am asking them to trace
a conversation, to make sense of what they're hearing and how
new perspectives change it, and then to reflect on their own
location, intents, and responsibilities as listeners. Like Jung,
who uses multigenre texts with this goal in mind, my aim is to
create a "participatory relationship between writer and reader,
a relationship that holds both responsible for the construction
of meaning" (Jung 2005, 34). Through the second question,
then, I hope students will begin to think about how the texts
and experiences of their lives shape their readings—and vice
versa. As they articulate a connection, they have the opportunity
to consider how their own experiences serve as frameworks for
their reading and at the same time, to consider how the readings may help them hear the stories of their lives differently.

While these questions help them approach our course texts
in a weblike relation to one another, a structure that creates
a more expansive network for understanding, I realized that
they also needed practice in listening for what is at stake for
the speaker/writer, and for the cultural logics that shape that
position (as well as their own). To begin this work, I borrowed a
practice that one of our TAs published in our Writing Teachers'
Sourcebook. The assignment is designed to help our first-year
students move beyond a rigid conception of argument as a
two-sided debate whose purpose is purely persuasion. Amber

Harris Leichner's assignment aims to emphasize multiplicity and what I see as a practice of "standing under" (Ratcliffe 1999) another's position.

Leichner invites her students to select an issue often deemed polarizing and then to research its multiple sides and the logics that inform them. She suggests that students ask the following questions about the stakeholders whose positions they have selected: "What do they believe? What are their basic assumptions about the issue? What is their history in relation to the issue? What are their goals, fears, and passions? What language do they use to 'frame' the issue?" I especially appreciate Amber's question about goals, fears, and passions, because even as she encourages students to research these positions, this question requires some "interpretive invention" about logics or perspectives that may not be explicit on the page. For instance, in the gun control dialogue I describe above, the political commentator mentioned the possible connections among the poor economy, resultant feelings of lack of control, and gun ownership. His idea was that when people are struggling financially, they feel less control in their daily lives, and they cling to things that give them the illusion of control—like owning a gun. Listening, then, for fears—and what might drive them—helps us to consider the problem more fully, and sometimes points us to a different problem altogether.

Leichner then moves students into a related project, inviting them to imagine a dialogue around a table or at a board meeting, wherein participants propose distinct and multiple positions. She asks the students to compose the proposals, deliberately examining the issue from a range of perspectives and showing readers "that each proposal deserves careful consideration." Then one student is to suggest a solution that the majority of the group might accept. The goal is to discover a space of shared ground, even among diverse positions.

Lamb describes a similar process in her 1991 essay, "Beyond Argument in Feminist Composition." She involves students in role-playing to move away from monologic argument and persuasion (understood as winning) as an end point and instead progress toward collaboration and negotiation. And in "Arguing Differently," Barry Kroll describes a course focused on alternate approaches to arguing in which he guided students through three papers that featured conciliatory (showing one has listened thoughtfully to the other side), integrative (locating shared ground even among differences), or deliberative strategies (considering multiple approaches to the same problem before arriving at a solution)—each challenging the default mode of adversarial argument (2005, 54).

While the goal for Leichner, Lamb, and Kroll is to revise normative approaches to argument, I wanted to make explicit the role of listening as part of engaging in debate and forming one's position. That is, I wanted to imagine what it meant to begin from a restored notion of logos—one equally dependent on listening and speaking—as an essential part of good argumentation (which my students differentiate from fighting). To this end, I called our first major project a "dialogic argument," or—as I framed it for my students—an argument that makes rhetorical listening visible. I describe it here not to promote it as the only way, or even an entirely successful way, to teach listening, but to offer an example that helped my students and me to better hear what rhetorical listening sounds like.

THE DIALOGIC ARGUMENT: LISTENING FIRST

I introduced the dialogic assignment to my students as an extension of our discussions on the role of listening and negotiation and as part of what we came to term "productive argumentation":

> Our recent readings have advocated for the importance of listening, mediation, and dialogue as important facets of argument. In this paper, you'll have the chance to employ some of these strategies. A dialogic argument is one that engages multiple sides of an issue, in an effort to learn from and negotiate with them. For this assignment, you will analyze—and put into dialogue—three different perspectives on a civic, cultural, or social issue that you would like to learn more about. That is, don't choose a topic about which your position is already fixed or decided. Or if you

do, please make sure you are willing to inquire into new perspectives. After analyzing both how the arguments are constructed and what interests and perspectives they articulate, you'll add your own voice to the conversation, reflecting on how listening to and situating yourself among three different perspectives has shaped your own position.

In helping them to think about their approach to the first part of the assignment, I offered these specific suggestions:

1. Locate three different perspectives (you can find these in article/essay/speech form or conduct your own interviews) on the issue, so that you can address the following questions:
   - What is the overarching problem?
   - What is the history of the issue?
   - What are the concerns of each perspective? How does this stakeholder articulate his or her concerns?
   - What does each perspective want or call for in regard to the issue? Why?
   - What are areas of agreement? Differences?

2. Consider in what form (and why) you want to represent these perspectives. You could use a traditional academic approach, offering a close reading and analysis of each perspective; you could create characters and compose a dialogue (trilogue!) among the stakeholders; you could describe each position in the form of an opinion column such as would be published in a newspaper, etc.

3. Please note: you may well have differences with the three perspectives you're engaging and want to critique them. Part 1, though, is the place for listening and articulating the range of positions. If you want to make a critique, it can come in part 2.

As I designed part 2, I deliberated over whether I should leave room for critique and contribution in the essay, knowing that within a diminished logos, both can serve as end points for discussion. That is, I didn't want my students to simply delay a predetermined thesis. My interest, instead, was in how these practices might change if they function in the context of repurposed listening. After all, rhetorical listening does not foreclose the necessity of critique. It does, however, call for a distinction between critique and discrediting, with the latter functioning as an end point, a dismissal, of the writer's words. Critique informed by listening, on the other hand, requires one to ask, "What's at stake? For whom? And why?" It recognizes the complexity of claims and positions as well as the specific manifold contexts that shape what and how one is able to hear. As Ratcliffe writes, "Such critique assumes the existence of multiple questions, multiple answers to each question, and multiple places from which to speak and listen" (Ratcliffe 2005, 97). It is this mode of critique, one that listens, that I wanted this assignment to promote.

Similarly, repurposed listening does not deny the importance of strong argument and positions. Rather, it fosters a different pathway to that argument, one that first acknowledges—and listens carefully to—the multiplicity and complexity that Ratcliffe describes. While I find practices like Lamb's, Leichner's, and Kroll's essays highly useful strategies for imagining mediation or negotiation, rather than persuasion, as the end point, my purpose was somewhat different: to consider what it means to come to a thoughtful contribution in the context of listening. This is how I framed the second part of the assignment. For this reason, I asked students to articulate their learning as part of framing their own contribution:

1. Consider what you have learned from engaging these three perspectives. Where do you find your own points of agreement, difference, or uncertainty?

2. Add your own voice to the dialogue, demonstrating how you are connecting with, departing from, and/or building upon the perspectives you've engaged. Here, then, you should reference the other sources in your response, indicating what elements of each perspective were particularly convincing (or not) to you and why. How is your own social location a factor? What is it about you as a listener that affects your interaction with each perspective? You might decide to take a strong stand on the issue; you might decide that additional research is necessary (as Anderson Cooper did in the video we watched on

the gun control debates); you might make a recommendation for a compromise.

3. The form for part 2 is also up to you; like any rhetorical decision, it should work to complement your purpose. If you've written the first part as a dialogue, you could go back and add your own voice to the conversation (if you do this, please turn in one version without your voice and then one with it). You could write a "position paper" or you own opinion column in response. You could write a letter to the three stakeholders you've studied. You could write a mock (or real) blog entry that addresses your learning about the issue and your response. I'm open to other ideas; feel free to run them by me.

While it did occur to me that the second part—after the discussion of learning—might take the form of a more traditional argument (a letter, position statement, and so on), my hope was that a serious undertaking of the process (recall that listening requires willingness) would alter, in some way, how the contribution looked and sounded. Before I turn to that student work, I want to illuminate a couple of notable moments that arose during group conferences when we discussed drafts focused on part 1 of the assignment. These moments placed into relief the normative mode of listening, which in some cases we needed to further unpack together before the student could do the work part 1 required.

First, at least five students had a difficult time locating three distinct perspectives. In a couple of cases, the draft established two positions (a for and an against), and then the student ceased composing. As I understood it, this didn't have to do with a lack of research or an inability to represent a perspective richly in writing—it had more to do with a conceptual framework of, or roadblock to, thinking beyond the two-sided debate. Here, the students' classmates were able to offer ideas for additional perspectives, but it also became clear that I should have included in the assignment the observation that sometimes stakeholders will hold the same "position" on an issue but for very different reasons. And sometimes a group of mostly like-minded people, or people who share a social category, will hold surprisingly different perspectives. Once it became clear that I should highlight this, it helped some move beyond a dualistic approach.

A related blockade to this work occurred when students got caught up in promoting one of the perspectives. In a couple of cases, the student represented the perspective he or she agreed with in much greater depth, or with much more fervor, than the others—sometimes at the expense of including other positions at all. Similarly, sometimes a writer offered a perspective in part 1 coupled with a strong critique of it. When I or a group member pointed out either of these moves, the students tended to laugh in recognition that they were so practiced at promoting a single view, they hadn't even realized they were veering from the assignment's call. I confessed that as a reader/listener, I often caught myself finding ways to help students strengthen certain positions (ones I agreed with, naturally) and had to think about my own listening intentions as well.

Part of the work of this project, then, came in the discussion about the process, which helped illuminate normative approaches to listening and prompted us to discuss together how to enact what Jung (2005) calls "writing that listens." I turn now to two projects that stood out in their enactment of listening, helping to make more audible how a restored logos might sound.

ARGUMENTS THAT LISTEN

For her dialogic argument, Calena Rudd, a junior psychology major, focused her inquiry on Internet censorship. The Benghazi attack that killed four Americans and was blamed on an anti-Islam YouTube video, served as one prompt for her inquiry; she also cited public concerns about bullying, discrimination, pornography, and military secret sharing. To consider the cultural context of this issue, Calena examined global practices of Internet censorship, learning that the United States is least restrictive in controlling Internet content, upholding the Federal Communication Commission's mission to "preserve the Internet as an open platform enabling consumer choice, freedom of expression, end-user control, competition, and the freedom to innovate without permission" (8.1 FCC). More restrictive countries, such as Iran and China, filter political, social, and military content as well as communication tools, but the United States has no such restrictions.

Calena then goes on to listen to three perspectives (offering multiple sources and rationales to flesh out each position) regarding Internet censorship: one favoring no government control of the Internet; one supporting "market censorship," with the idea that more voices—or, we might say, competition and critique—prevent the entrenchment of uniform views (here, among other sources, she cites Project Censored, whose mission is "to teach students and the public about the role of a free press in a free society—and to tell the News That Didn't Make the News and Why."); and one promoting regulation (here she notes that child pornography is raised as a common argument). The careful work Calena did in considering the stakes and concerns of each perspective can also be heard in part 2 of her essay, where she grapples with her own position in the form of a letter to all of those whose perspectives she engages. She begins the letter by addressing what she views as common ground, including protection of children, one-sided news stories, and leakage of military secrets. Then she writes, "I began by building off [our] common ground to investigate all three of your stances on this issue. I thought my questions would be answered and I would conclude my analysis with a solid and bold opinion on one specific side of the issue. This is not the case."

She then goes on to specifically address each perspective, noting where they have common ground and articulating her remaining questions. For instance, of those who promote complete Internet freedom, she asks how to resolve the issue of child pornography and how to ensure our children are protected from exploitation. Of those who promote self-censorship (or a multiplicity of perspectives), she commends a project that offers alternative images of women's beauty and then moves on to articulate her remaining concerns. She writes:

> To you, Sifat Azad, I would like to show my gratitude for your courage to share the harmful effects of the media upon women. As a young woman, I know that I am easily bombarded with negative images of who I should be and lies about my purpose as a woman. I agree that we should fight back [against] these lies by offering alternative sights and images of women who are authentically beautiful (*PolicyMic*). My only concern with self-censorship is what about pornography, military secrets, or online predators? Can we not impose laws to make these actions illegal? (Rudd 2013)

To those who advocate for Internet regulation, she finds common ground in the desire to remove hateful and misleading messages. Calena draws upon her location as a person of Christian faith to identify with those who were affected by the aforementioned video mocking Muhammad. Here, though, her own position begins to emerge more clearly. She writes, "I too want my faith to be protected from lies and slander. Yet, this is simply impossible. I cannot regulate others' beliefs, thoughts, and speech any more than I can regulate what they post online" (Rudd 2013).

Calena goes on to articulate that it is likewise impossible to censor "offensive" material, since there is no agreement on what is considered offensive. Finally, she addresses the aim of protecting children, finding common ground with those who argue for use of Internet controls in schools and libraries. In the end, though, she determines that it is the very availability of these perspectives that allowed her to explore this issue in the first place. While she does not come to what she dubs a "solid, bold opinion," her writing enacts an effort to stand under other perspectives, to consider her own locations (as a young woman, a Catholic), and to use listening as a way to more deeply consider a problem and potential responses—not simply to win. The dialogic essay, in fact, served as an entryway to her final project, in which she composed a blog that continued to highlight perspectives on Internet censorship, adding her own developing ideas to the ongoing discussion.

Jennifer Swenson, another student in the course, began with an issue that she already had formed opinions about, but she didn't allow her stance to limit her willingness to listen. Jennifer's paper begins with a narrative about Michael, a student in her mother's first-grade classroom at a magnet school in Omaha, Nebraska. Michael is an English-language learner (ELL); Spanish is his first language. He is having difficulty understanding even simple instructions in the classroom. In kindergarten, Jennifer explains, he was taught in a bilingual classroom, but his family needed to move due to a change in circumstances; his current school offers no such option. Jennifer quotes her mother: "'I don't think he has any learning disabilities. I actually think he's a really smart kid, and he could thrive in a bilingual classroom,' Mom said, 'but we just can't give him the support he needs, and there probably isn't enough room for him at other schools'" (Swenson 2013). Jennifer's piece, then, features the role of bilingual education in the United States.

To lay the groundwork for her inquiry, she explains how bilingual education typically works, offers the rationale for such programs—including research from the Institute for Language and Education Policy that indicates ELLs perform better in such classrooms—and then explains that program funding has been cut severely in recent years. No Child Left Behind dismantled the Bilingual Education Act, which had provided federal support for bilingual education, instead allocating funding to more traditional total-immersion programs.

Jennifer goes on to explore three perspectives. Here, though, she moves outside of a for-or-against approach to bilingual education to instead examine the differing cultural logics that shape the three stances she considers. To describe the first, she cites James Crawford, the president of the Institute for Language and Education Policy. He supports bilingual education as the best way to ensure equal education opportunities, but argues that this pedagogical movement suffers from a "public relations issue" centered on the assumption that the use of one's native language is not only a diversion from English acquisition but culturally "divisive"—a threat to American values and unity (Swenson 2013). Indeed, as Jennifer moves on to two positions that advocate for instruction in English only, she shows how this issue is deeply tied to cultural assumptions about what constitutes belonging in American culture. For instance, she quotes the English First website, which states that "it is impossible to fully live the American dream without a working knowledge of English both in reading and speaking." This view is supported by Senator James Inhofe of Oklahoma, who has repeatedly introduced legislation to make English the "national language" and to require that government business be conducted only in English (Swenson 2013).

Jennifer then moves on to listen to another view that supports English-only teaching, but this time from the immigrant perspective. Mauro Mujica, an immigrant from Chile, argues for English-only legislation because he believes there is a direct link between English acquisition and success in the classroom and workplace (Swenson 2013). Jennifer comes to see a distinction, then, between those who support English only based on a perceived threat to American culture and those, like Mujica, who support it because they believe it is a pathway to inclusion.

In the second part of the essay, in which Jennifer contributes her own perspective, she remarks on her surprise in coming across Mujica's perspective, describing how it altered her own thinking:

> Because people like Inhofe and English First often make such inflammatory statements, their voices are often heard above other, more reasonable arguments on the side of official English . . . But then I encountered the article advocating official English that was written by Mujica, which absolutely shocked me. He clearly supports endorsing English as an official language, because he believes it will ultimately benefit immigrants like him. He raises legitimate concerns about the ability of immigrants to succeed in America without knowing English, and frames the issue in such a way that leads readers to think that to disavow official English policies is to deny immigrants the tools they need to carve out a place in American society. It's a shame that Mujica's voice is effectively drowned out by the much more controversial remarks of Inhofe and English First. (Swenson 2013)

Jennifer then emphasizes a need to listen more closely to those who occupy the center of this debate—immigrants and educators. How, for instance, are immigrants acculturated in dominant discourse of inclusion and patriotism? How might their perspectives complicate, challenge, or enrich dominant modes of thinking? Likewise, she notes, teachers' voices, like her mother's, are too often drowned out by the "prioritization of acculturation over education." She argues for a reframing of the question that drives this debate, moving away from "How can we make these children American?" to ask instead "What is the best way to ensure that all children in America have access to an education that will allow them to be successful?" (Swenson 2013).

While Jennifer's is an exceptionally astute paper, she wasn't the only one to conclude, as a result of listening to multiple perspectives of an issue, that particular—often quite important—voices are drowned out or excluded from cultural debate. We have learned, after all, to listen for dualisms and to attend most to the voices that are the most strident, inflammatory, or culturally valued. Consequently, many students focused their second major project on spotlighting those less-heard voices, showing how listening differently, and listening to different voices, creates opportunity for richer dialogue—which is the very purpose of rhetorical listening.

THE RISK OF RHETORICAL LISTENING

If listening has historically served as the feminine counterpart to masculine speech acts, neoliberal listening training appropriates those feminized characteristics—understanding, empathy, support—to ends that bolster existing social structures and dynamics. Neither the value assigned to listening nor the outcome of listening is revised. To listen from a divided logos is to listen from a secure, stable position. To listen from a restored logos, on the other hand, is to repurpose listening toward an openness to movement, and to the possibility of hearing from a position that is uncomfortable, disconcerting, or tenuous.

In promoting what they call "serious argumentation," which involves careful consideration of the words and positions of others, Dennis Lynch, Diana George, and Marilyn Cooper note the risks involved: "The risk is not merely that your social position and identity may be challenged, or not merely that someone may disagree with your intellectual position, or not even that you may lose the argument; the risk is also that you may become different than you were before the argument began" (Lynch, George, and Cooper 1997, 68). This, I would argue, is both the risk and the purpose of rhetorical listening—the risk of reading, writing, and thinking outside of a predetermined position, even as we question and rethink the positions we inevitably bring to our exchanges with others' words.

And with risk comes possibility of gain. Here, the gain is not corporate profit, though rhetorical listening may well be useful in business as well as academic settings; it is rather the new knowledge possibilities and practices that emerge from genuinely listening to voices too often muted, a listening that disrupts the power dynamics that contributed to their silencing in the first place.

In the next chapter I focus on another way neoliberal values contribute to silencing, as I examine how neoliberal standardization not only excludes teacher voices but also removes embodied, local knowledge from educational discourse. Feminist knowledges, I argue, help us discover possibilities for embodied, located agency.

NOTE

1.   Thanks to teaching colleagues Chris Gallagher and Lesley Bartlett, who helped me articulate these questions.

4

REPURPOSING AGENCY
From Standardized to Located

One afternoon in my Composition Theory and Practice class, a seminar for new TAs, a white male TA described a lively discussion that had transpired in his class. He had invited his first-year composition students to "read him as a rhetorical text." His impetus was to show them that everything is an argument, including the clothing one wears, the choice to sit or stand, the haircut one chooses. The TA seemed a bit taken aback when a young woman interjected, "I could *never* do that in my class." She explained that as a woman, she had to navigate being read as an object on a daily basis, and the last thing she wanted to do was invite her students to make her body a primary text in the classroom.

From here, a compelling conversation unfolded about the role of our bodies in the classroom—what they reveal (or we fear they reveal) about us, and what markers we assume will undercut or facilitate the teacher's authority or agency. Our discussion exposed the habitual conflation of agency and neutrality, underscoring the (mis)conception that an authoritative teaching subject is "unmarked"—or in other words, marked with masculinity, whiteness, (seemingly) unaccented English, and so on. This view relies on a Western, monolithic view of agency that is "single-dimensional" and "unidirectional" (Maitra 2013, 366); this neoliberal agency, as I'll refer to it, presumably allows one to *possess* authority and exert control over oneself and others, independent of contexts. Acquiring agency within neoliberal contexts requires that one occupy the dominant authoritative subjectivity and succeed within established relations of power.

Indeed, feminist scholars Miriam David and Sue Clegg contend that neoliberal values replace embodied actors with

DOI: 10.7330/9781607323884.c004

"individualized, decontextualized, competitive neoliberal sub-jects" (David and Clegg 2008, 488). This dynamic is evident in education researcher Louise Archer's study of how new faculty members construct professional identity within increasingly neoliberal universities. Although she studies universities in the United Kingdom, the responses certainly resonate in the United States as well. For instance, her respondents describe the privileging of a "'macho' competitive ethos" demonstrated by quantifiable markers—grant money, high evaluation scores, and number of publications. In this audit culture prizing indi-vidualism and competitive practices, respondents note that creativity and risk taking, as well as collaboration and colle-giality, often become casualties (Archer 2008, 272–273). Her respondents are simultaneously critical of neoliberal values and resigned to them, as many describe attachment to "producing dominantly valued output" and a "discourse of accountability," which they view as distinguishing the more productive present from the past. The alternative, these new faculty members sug-gest, would result in laziness (of faculty) and lack of order and productivity (272). A neoliberal culture, then, becomes the only reasonable and conceivable choice, with agency gained by accli-mation to and success within it.

The new faculty members' fluency in neoliberal discourse, Archer notes, does not simply reflect the current cultural context but it is "constitutive and productive" (Archer 2008, 272). This discourse teaches us whom to be and how to belong in (and to) this setting, and in so doing, privileges a seemingly "standard" neoliberal subject: one who is rational, competitive, autonomous, and productive. This decontextualized individual is assumed to compete on a level playing field, which occludes attention to particular embodied subjects and the complex contexts in which they work—not to mention the student subjects whom they teach. And the notion that anybody can compete and win rei-fies an "ungendered but masculinist" culture—one that covers its masculinist values with neutrality (David and Clegg 2008, 494).

Consequently, even as marginalized groups of fac-ulty and students have increased access to postsecondary education—something neoliberal measures hold up as a mark of inclusivity and diversity—the structures and practices of privilege often remain unchecked. The result is a what queer feminist scholars Richard Jones Jr. and Bernadette Calafell call a "corporate multiculturalism," wherein diversity is embraced so long as it is marketable, entertaining, and unproblematic (Jones and Calafell 2012, 964). The burden, then, lies on individuals to acclimate to the existing structures of the institution, since they will be accepted only to the extent, as Jones and Calafell put it, that they remain "docile, unthreatening, and invested in self-commodification" (969). In the neoliberal model, self-commodification and acclimation—belonging in and to the dominant structure—serve as the pathway to agency. For marginalized subjects, employing neoliberal agency often requires the denial of one's embodied location, knowledge, and history.

Feminist scholars, alternatively, have long promoted a different means to agency—one that involves embracing a marginal position as a source of knowledge and authority. From a wide span of disciplinary perspectives, feminist scholars including Patricia Hill Collins (1986), Adrienne Rich (1986), and bell hooks (1990) argue that the margins offer a keener view of dominant structures and that articulating located, embodied knowledge is a channel both to examine epistemological possibilities and to take responsibility for the partiality of one's perspective. These arguments offer a revised mode of *enacting* agency that insists upon illuminating traits obscured by neoliberalism: embodiment, location, and responsibility to and connection with one another. Indeed, as Maitra argues, feminist agency requires one to "formulate choices" rather than to unreflexively choose among existing options. Formulating choices involves a conscious consideration of "not just how things are but of how they *could* be." This cannot be discerned, however, without careful attention to social contexts, locations, and histories. Maitra acknowledges that a discussion of women's choices in the context of these factors "gets very complex"; nevertheless, she argues that "any viable discussion of agency in feminism" must "address this complexity" (Maitra 2013, 361). And so rather than assuming that agency stems from acclimation to dominant structures, a feminist agency interrogates the dominant modes and practices that constitute belonging (Rowe 2005) in the first place so as to illuminate possibilities for alternative ways of moving in and among our locations.

In what follows, I argue for repurposing neoliberal agency as *located* agency, a practice that includes examining, valuing, and taking responsibility for our locations and that opens possibilities for marginalized locations to serve as resources for teaching, learning, and knowing. Because enacting authority is such an important, and often fraught, part of teacher learning, I focus in particular on highlighting located agency with new teachers of composition. I offer a way to help new TAs articulate and enact a located agency that does not require mere assimilation to neoliberal structures but instead allows them to see the possibilities that emerge from the nexus of their subjectivities, locations, and relations.

NEOLIBERAL STANDARDIZATION AND TEACHER AGENCY

Feminist scholar Anna Feigenbaum argues that neoliberal structures trap both educators and students in a dynamic that "maintains the corporate fantasy of relation without flesh and encounter without touch" (Feigenbaum 2007, 340). Indeed, at both the K–12 and, increasingly, post-secondary level of education, we see efforts to standardize teaching and learning in ways that remove teacher (and student) bodies, knowledge, and commitments. Take, for instance, distance learning courses, in which curriculum "experts" design the content, and interchangeable contingent instructors deliver it; machine-scored writing that, as the NCTE statement warns, removes written communication's purpose "to create human interactions through a complex, socially consequential system of meaning making" (NCTE Task Force on Writing Assessment 2013); and assessment measures that are designed by corporations, not local educators. In these situations, teachers serve as little more than technicians. They deliver prepackaged, standardized knowledge much as a

Starbucks barista delivers a uniform latte, no matter where she, or the store, is located.

Within these cultures of standardization, belonging involves ascribing to a set of normative practices and values that results in a uniform product. As Cochran-Smith and Lytle note, in settings ranging from K–12 schools to college teacher development to administrator programs, the "competent practitioner" is "self-sufficient, certain, and independent" (Cochran-Smith and Lytle 2009, 114). This certainty is thought to come from acquisition of "what works" practices, sanctioned knowledge, and management skills—all of which are designed to ensure a smooth transaction that achieves predetermined outcomes. This, again, is the fantasy of "relation without flesh and encounter without touch" (Feigenbaum 2007, 340).

While this transaction-centered model of education is certainly shaped by and enacted through technologies, assessment mechanisms, and legislation (like No Child Left Behind), Feigenbaum highlights the role of neoliberal *individualism* on which this fantasy depends. This conception of individualism calls for a competitive, autonomous subject and dictates "appropriate" pedagogies that rest on the assumption of education as a disembodied, rational exchange (2007, 340). Context, difference, and embodiment are papered over by narratives of excellence, efficiency, and productivity. And excellence, as Patricia Harkin reminds us, refers to "competition, and its referent is winning" (2006, 31). Its agent, then, is the competitor, who plays the game by the rules and produces valued, quantifiable results.

Within this framework, it is assumed that "winning"— or achieving the right "output" (degrees, tenure and promotion, grants, publications)—imbues one with neoliberal agency, understood as a state of being, something one owns (and presumably deserves). It is often viewed as a state that differentiates one from others, functioning as a power over them. It is not surprising, then, that the new TAs with whom I work are preoccupied with whether they "have" agency. It is also understandable, because this view promises that one day, the uncertainty of teaching will evaporate; there will be no doubt—given her position, her degree, her list of publications, and so on—that the teacher has agency or authority over her students. Of course, subjects who occupy marginalized identities know that this "merit-based" approach to agency is a fiction; titles and degrees do not negate markers of gender, race, sexual orientation, and disability, nor do they nullify contexts of discrimination or oppression.

Indeed, neoliberal discourses would have us believe that individuals, not values or structures, are in need of change—and often, that individuals are best served by acclimation to a more standard mode of being and doing. Because neoliberal conceptions of whom to be, how that mode is enacted, and what is desired are so commonly repeated, adhering to them becomes not only the norm but the only "rational" option. For this reason, as Bronwyn Davies et al. argue, we need to be aware of how neoliberalism, as a "new dominant discourse," may "take us over, reinscribe us, transform us, without us having realized that it was in urgent need of deconstruction and resistance" (Davies et al. 2006, 100). Feminist repurposing of neoliberal agency and individualism requires us to illuminate and critique the "constitutive force" of neoliberal discourse (99) as a first step to discovering alternative possibilities. It further highlights the limitations—for both teachers and students—of conceiving of authority as something earned and held rather than something socially inscribed and enacted within particular contexts.

To that end, I draw from feminist rhetorician Aimee Carrillo Rowe's call to interrogate our "modes of belonging," a process that prompts us to articulate the "conditions and effects of inclusion within various sites of belonging" (Rowe 2005, 28). Here, she is interested in how we are made into particular kinds of subjects through the acceptance of certain invitations or requirements and the rejection of others. She draws upon Louis Althusser's notion of being "hailed," wherein the police officer calls a subject with a "Hey, you there" that requires the subject to submit to a particular role in a web of power. We are "hailed" or interpellated all the time, of course, into particular roles or identities—which come to seem normal and natural—and our answers often determine our belonging. She is interested in possibilities for resisting hegemonic belonging. Drawing from Chela Sandoval's (2000) concept of "reverse interpellation," Rowe aims to illuminate the "politics at stake" in our belonging. Who is allowed to belong in this context? How is belonging enacted and demonstrated? Who may belong with most ease? Who must alter herself to belong? How might we imagine and enact alternative modes of belonging?

The aforementioned example of "corporate multiculturalism" offers a ripe example for interrogating the politics of belonging. On the surface, the university may exhibit a visible commitment to increasing diversity through statements on job ads, images on websites, or curricular outcomes. Offering an invitation, however, is not the same as creating the conditions for belonging; presence is not the same as agency. Answering to the "Hey, you there" of university belonging often requires one to self-regulate and to perform within hegemonic boundaries. But there is also a possibility for agency in questioning the conditions of belonging, and this allows us to become participants in our own making and reflexive about the process—and in so doing, we foster alliances with others. As Rowe writer, "The ways in which hegemonic discourses 'hail' us as subjects can thus be rethought through belonging; not only in terms of how power hails us, but also the ways in which power may be hailed by us as a resistive reinscription" (Rowe 2005, 28). For Rowe and other feminist thinkers, this means agency begins with—not apart from—one's specific, embodied location. I turn now to feminist arguments that view marginalized locations as sites of resistance, creativity, and imagination—as building blocks for enacting agency differently.

A VIEW FROM THE BODY: LOCATED AGENCY

Adrienne Rich's "Notes toward a Politics of Location" marks a turning point in feminist theory toward a situated reflexivity, a concept that is vital to a repurposing agency. In the essay, Rich acknowledges a universalizing tendency in feminist theorizing, including her own, to overlook difference among women with regard to race, class, educational status, and sexuality; as a result, abstractness is privileged over particular embodiment. In contrast, she calls for a recognition of location, of specificity, that requires us to "name the ground we're coming from" and "the conditions we have taken for granted" (Rich 1986, 219). She moves, then, from the universal, standard, and abstract to the particular, calling readers to do the same, by beginning with "the geography closest in—the body" (212).

The body, though, has multiple identities, and our locations both allow and hinder our belonging, include and exclude, empower and oppress, often at the same time. As Rich maps her locations—female, white, Jewish, a mother, a writer—she observes that locating herself in her body means more than identifying it as biologically female; it means "recognizing this white skin, the places it has taken me, the places it has not let me go" (1986, 216). For Rich, attending to one's politics of location involves accepting responsibility for the locations of our knowledge, and for what those locations allow and hinder, make visible and hide. Implicit in this work is the recognition that knowledge is always partial, always perspectival—something neoliberal approaches and their standardized mechanisms gloss over or disguise.

This limitation to the partial, however, is not viewed as a detriment or, as Nedra Reynolds puts it, a "block to the 'truth' to be eliminated," but instead serves as a reminder for us "to see differently, to shift position, to make adjustments" (Reynolds 1993, 332). It prompts us to ask: what is lost by the marginalizing of some perspectives and the universalizing of others? Feminist scholars, in fact, contend that a marginalized position can be repurposed as a site of agency. For instance, bell hooks argues that there is a difference between marginality that is "imposed by oppressive structures" and marginality that one "chooses as a site of resistance—as a location of radical openness and possibility" (hooks 1990, 153). This is a choice she deems necessary: as a black girl in a small Kentucky town, she learns what it means to cross the railroad tracks into a white world, where she can enter as an observer, an outsider, but may not live. "Living as we did—on the edge—we developed a particular way of seeing reality. We looked both from the outside in and from the inside out. We focused our attention on the center as well as on the margin. We understood both." From this perspective, hooks writes, she developed a way of seeing unknown to her oppressors, a way that "sustained us, aided us in our struggle to transcend poverty and despair, strengthened our sense of self and solidarity" (149). This is the marginality she chooses, one that serves as a site of creativity, imagination, and resistance. This choice of marginality serves as a useful example of Maitra's notion of a "formulated" choice. It is the result of careful attention to social contexts and histories (how things are), with a keen eye on new possibilities (how things could be) (Maitra 2013, 361).

When hooks later enters a predominantly white university, her mother warns, "You can take what the white people have to offer, but you do not have to love them." Hooks eventually comes to understand that her mother's words were not about denying love to people of other races; rather, she was insisting upon her daughter's agency in separating useful, life- and work-enhancing knowledge from ways of knowing (or belonging) that would lead to "estrangement, alienation, and worse—assimilation and co-optation." Her mother knew, hooks writes, that she would be "tried," or made to feel that the only way to "make it" was to buy fully into dominant culture. But that wasn't the only available path. Hooks writes, "She was reminding me of the necessity of opposition and simultaneously encouraging me not to lose that radical perspective shaped and formed by marginality" (hooks 1990, 150). Here, knowledge created on the margins is viewed as a resource for counter-hegemonic knowledge, creativity, and possibility. But valuing the margin as a resource does not mean one must stay on the margins; rather, it means enacting alternative modes of belonging and creating alternative spaces, allowing one to claim knowledge, practices, and locations that are devalued by dominant structures and to simultaneously seek new knowledge and experience (148).

Just as hooks's mother advises that she work within and against white university culture, Rowe argues for a practice of "differential belonging" that highlights and creates possibilities for alternative enactments of belonging. Extending Chela Sandoval's notion of "differential resistance," Rowe outlines four conditions of belonging, or ways of organizing social relations for marginalized subjects: *assimilationist*, which involves deemphasizing difference in order to be recognized as equals by those in power; *revolutionary*, in which difference is used as a vehicle for critique of the current social structure; *supremacist*, whereby a group's differences are regarded as a better way of knowing or relating than are dominant modes, and are thus potentially transformative; and *separatist*, a mode of belonging that offers "an important site to dream, to create visions and try them on with others who begin with similar assumptions, politics and experiences." Differential belonging recognizes fluidity among these modes, and each may be necessary depending on the moment, situation, and dynamics at play. But *agency*, as Rowe sees it, emerges in the movement among them. "Becoming stuck in any mode or seeing modes as mutually exclusive can be counterproductive. It is precisely the movement across these modes that allows us to be politically productive" (Rowe 2005, 34). Enacting one mode of belonging can fuel, provide insight to, or critique another; drawing from multiple modes can offer possibilities that a single mode would occlude.

Together, these feminist scholars make a case for location as both embodied and enacted. That is, a located agency takes seriously both the limitations and possibilities that emerge from our material, embodied locations and knowledges, attending to how our geographic and institutional locations shape what is doable at any given moment. But unlike neoliberal agency, which is accessible only to those who can belong, compete, and win within a rigid set of rules (which are nevertheless framed as universal), a located agency provides a more expansive set of choices about how to navigate those dynamics, such that possibility can be drawn from the margins as well as the center and from movement among different modes of belonging. This is where the importance of enactment emerges.

Rowe argues, for instance, that "politics of location" approaches may inadvertently fix identities or group belongings in a way that "erases the choices that we make around our belongings which are constitutive of our identities" (2005, 32). That is, if we think of our locations as made up of fixed identities (for example, I am a woman; I am a midwesterner; I am white), we lose an opportunity to reflect on how the choices we make to enact our belonging may exclude and oppress as well as to consider how we might act in new ways that disrupt habitual modes. This is particularly pertinent to privileged locations, like whiteness, which become both invisible and compulsory, such that both white people and people of color are expected to fall inside its norms. As Rowe contends, "Invisibility undermines agency; we cannot alter that which we cannot see" (30). Indeed, once these modes of belonging are made visible, we can imagine ways to disrupt and challenge them and to enact more expansive modes.

While heeding Rowe's warning about the risk of fixing locations, however, I hold that in a time when neoliberal discourses fetishize standardization and deny local contexts, it is crucial that we emphasize location, which I understand to encompass a dynamic interplay among embodiment, social spaces (institutional and cultural), and the relations that animate them. If we do not pay adequate attention to location, both material, embodied location and the specific contexts that simultaneously enable and prohibit our enactments, it is too easy to slip back into neoliberal assumptions of level playing fields and individual autonomy. I am drawn, for instance, to the metaphor Sandoval and Rowe employ, wherein differential belonging and resistance function like a clutch in a manual transmission automobile, allowing the driver to decide in each moment how to deploy the engine's power. But it's also necessary to observe the road, conditions both internal and external to the car, the speed limit—and the relationship of the driver to those circumstances. Is the driver a person of color in Arizona, at risk of being read as an illegal immigrant? A white woman in a Lexus or minivan driving down a suburban street? An African American male driving down that same suburban street? One's deployment of the engine is always dependent on locations: embodied, geographic, and geopolitical.

Enacting a located agency, then, takes into account differential belonging and pays close attention to the subject as always in relation to other subjects and to the specific contexts in which she or he lives and works. Ultimately, as I'll show, located agency not only serves the actor but extends outward to deepen and expand ways of knowing, knowledge practices, and connections among subjects. In the next section, I turn toward the work of facilitating located agency with the TAs in our pedagogy seminar, as they navigate belonging in this new role.

TEACHER LEARNING AND LOCATED AGENCY

In my interactions with new TAs, I'm aware of a pervasive, almost tangible, anxiety that seems to increase as job prospects in English decrease. There is fear about job security—in this case, a teaching assistantship; there is fear about the inevitable "messiness" of pedagogy, especially as it relates to their evaluations (by students and administrators). But there are other—not, I would argue, unrelated—concerns: what if my students don't see me as an authority? What if my (insert: queer, female, raced, transgendered, foreign, working-class, pregnant) body is not read as standard enough? Or is conflated—as we know our bodies often are—with the pedagogy or with the teacher's stance? The assumption is that anything other than a neutral stance will be read as a detriment. The teacher is too political, too female, too queer, and the like, with "too" marking an excessive subjectivity in need of discipline. My aim, then, is to help them consider how embodied, situated knowledge may be a resource for, not a detriment to, agency.

One way I introduce notions of located agency is by teaching texts in which instructors highlight their processes of navigating and challenging proscriptive teacher identities. Often it is necessary to first illuminate the regulatory practices of normative "belonging" as a university instructor. Karen Kopelson's discussion of her attempt to enact strategic neutrality helps us excavate these assumptions. In her essay "Of Ambiguity and Erasure: The Perils of Performance Pedagogy," Kopelson notes that because she is "a walking stereotype" of a lesbian, she assumes she is an "easy read" for her students and therefore carefully constructs a pedagogy "that works within and against what I consider to be my identity's glaringly evident markers" (Kopelson 2006, 563). That is, she performs a strategic neutrality to help ward off assumptions that she is promoting an agenda that corresponds with her embodied identity. Her hope is that this strategy will facilitate her students' receptivity to those political issues she does discuss in the course. And it seems to work. Kopelson reads her students' glowing evaluations, which remark on an open and respectful classroom environment, as verification of this approach. "Wow, I think, time and again, semester after semester, because this little production of mine is an encore performance, this ambiguity/neutrality show sure goes over big; *they like me; they really like me!*" (565). But then Kopelson complicates her own performance, sharing a story about a student who was shocked to see her with a female partner at a local bar; she realizes that she may have inadvertently "erased" her identity as a gay subject. "I meant to perform my savvy neutrality . . . I did not, however, mean to *disappear*" (566). In the end she contemplates, without offering any answers or advice, the act of coming out—in whatever form that takes—as necessarily rhetorical, dependent on "context, intention, and audience reception" (569).

This piece is often pivotal for my students, serving to illuminate the idealized "standard" subject in the contemporary classroom, where the teacher is expected to function as a "palatable product" who does not disrupt the illusion of neutrality (Weber 2010). While the TAs I work with also want to offer students an atmosphere in which they feel respected and heard—and are keenly attuned to what their students might articulate in course evaluations—this piece prompts us to ask: is a respectful atmosphere contingent upon perceived neutrality? Who or what is most often regarded as neutral? What are the costs, for Kopelson and for us as teachers and learners, of performing neutrality? For whom is a neutral performance most accessible or possible? For whom is it impossible?

Engaging this piece, then, is one avenue to illuminate the expectations of the neoliberal subject—the modes of belonging deemed necessary to "fit in" as university instructors and future professors. Along with Kopelson's text, I also point students to scholarly examples that depict what I view as located agency. Here, teachers assess their own subjectivities in relation to local contexts and then discern possibilities for examining embodied knowledge as a resource—while also acknowledging the risks that accompany this work.[1] For instance, in their essay "Coming Out Pedagogy: Risking Identity in Language and Literature Classrooms," Brueggemann and Moddelmog explore the relationships, "both oppressive and enabling, between what has been *named* (a position of identity as an absolute) and what has been *claimed* (a position of identity as contingent)" (Brueggemann and Moddelmog 2003, 213; my emphasis). Thus, on the first day of class Brueggemann identifies herself as deaf, a move that helps her create effective classroom communication and address any necessary classroom modifications, but it also begins to challenge normative conceptions of deaf individuals (her named identity). She explains what she can and cannot hear (that it is not a simple matter of silence versus sound) and how she navigates communication practices with technology, lipreading, reliance on context clues, and body language. She then moves from identifying what she calls "functional reasons" for naming her disability to "ethically *claiming* a disability identity" (214; my emphasis). Here, she replaces deaf with "hard-of-hearing," which not only more accurately defines her experience but also "represents a hyphenated existence," challenging solid categories of belonging. She writes, "I am not (that) old; I do use (some) sign language, although not here in the Ohio State University English classroom; I clearly am speaking (and don't deaf people have trouble speaking?); I look (pretty) normal; and I am, after all, the teacher (the voice and body of authority), am I not?" (214–215).

The parenthetical phrases break the repetition of normative roles and, she notes, they spark questions on the part of her students, as they begin to think differently about what it means to be disabled or able-bodied, and how these are temporary and fluid states, existing in relationship to other social locations. Brueggemann, for instance, explains that had she not been white and middle class, she may not have been mainstreamed in school and allowed the academic path she pursued. The practice of claiming this marginalized identity—what could easily be characterized as a detriment—allows her both to draw agency from her location and to help her students consider how institutions (for example, family, medicine, religion, education) and normalizing discourses shape our identities (Brueggemann and Moddelmog 2003, 229). Students may ask, for instance, what hyphenated identities do I live and enact? Where is there a tension between how I am categorized (as a rural student, a Christian, a Latino, a fraternity member) and how I enact this aspect of my identity? In what ways might this tension be explored? How might it lend me agency or ethos?

For the students in my Composition Theory and Practice seminar, texts like Brueggemann and Moddelmog's serve to highlight the possibilities—for cultural critique, for expanding notions of agency, for relating to others—that emerge from valuing our embodied locations as integral to teaching and learning and, in so doing, disrupt normative conceptions of belonging. While new teachers may choose to address their embodied locations differently, or not at all, we are served by acknowledging that our bodies do, for better and for worse, make meaning in the classroom. As Scott Andrew Smith writes, "Perhaps what we carry into the classroom physically—our way of carrying ourselves but also the ways in which our bodies have carried us or let us down—is just as important as the books and syllabi that we carry in our hands and the theories and ideas we carry in our heads" (Smith 2003, 32). Working toward a located agency means helping new teachers consider how the bodies we carry—whether we deem them burdens or resources or both—and the locations we live and enact are part of how we know, and consequently, deserve consideration as we examine how we want to sponsor the knowledge of others.

POSSIBILITIES FOR TEACHER AGENCY

In addition to engaging others' navigation of agency, TAs also need room to consider their own locations as a valid option for intellectual work. While this is never something I require, several students each semester—typically those for whom navigating their embodied or marked identity has felt fraught—choose to examine issues of location and agency in their "Pedagogical Insights" essay. I model this essay after those included in the reader *Relations, Locations, Positions: Composition Theory for Writing Teachers* (Vandenberg, Hum, and Clary-Lemon 2006), in which teachers describe how the composition theories they engage animate their work in the classroom with students and show how teaching is also theory making. I describe the project's goals in this way:

> This piece should draw both from published sources (at least four) and from the text of your classroom. That is, it should both locate your question/issue *within the context of an existing conversation* and offer a meaningful, engaged *contribution* to it, based on your reading, reflection, and experience. It should also show how the *integration of theory and practice* furthers your thinking—and, so doing, it should *prompt further thinking for others*.

Although early in the semester, many of the TAs fear they will have no such insight to offer, by the end, they certainly do—and for those I turn to now, they come to see that these insights are achieved as a result of articulating their locations and discovering how location may serve as a site of agency.

As does Brueggemann, my students often describe the navigation of teacher authority as beginning on the first day of class, when the teacher enters the classroom and wonders whether she or he will be recognized as such. Here, Monica describes her own navigation—literally and figuratively:

The sound of a small motor carries down the old basement hall-way, passing like a shadow into every classroom. Students sitting in desks of their first college semester hear the hum, unsure of what it is until it rolls through the door frame. They might think the occupant is a fellow student as they pull desks to clear a path for her. She crosses the room, parking behind a table at the front, under the wall-to-wall whiteboard. Jaws do not drop. When the time is right, she introduces herself—her name, her year, and focus of study in the master's program in the depart-ment. She passes around an introductory writing course syllabus. Nothing about height or motors is mentioned. (Rentfrow 2009)

While Monica notes that she had no choice but to "come out" to her students on the first day—"being a little person half dependent upon her scooter, there was no opting to 'hide' my 'disability'"—it wasn't until later in the semester that she explic-itly acknowledged dwarfism as part of her identity. She did so by modeling her public writing assignment with a pamphlet she designed to raise awareness about the national organization Little People of America, Inc. In her essay, she gives two reasons for her moment of "claiming" her identity as disabled. First, she wants to provide students a "tangible example" of how we can make arguments from our commitments, passions, and loca-tions. But second, she writes that to ignore her dwarfism feels false, especially as she reflects on how her family taught her to "be strong and humble enough to find ways of working with the world." For Monica, this means both showing her students how her embodied location could be used as a "tool for learning in the classroom" and acknowledging that it sometimes meant she had to ask her students for assistance. She jokes, "I do not ever pretend as if I can go-go-Gadget my arm up to pull down the projection screen."

Monica also describes wrestling with the question of whether acknowledging her disability might undermine her students' sense of her as a traditional authority. She considers Smith's perspective in "On the Desk: Dwarfism, Teaching, and the Body." Smith chooses not to discuss his physicality in the classroom: "No student in my nine years of being on that table at the head of the class has ever asked me to explain the paragraphs of my legs or the thesis statement of my dwarfism . . . No one has yet to break that silence fully and completely, and I am not sure I want it broken any more than I want students to ask me about my holiday plans or what I do for fun on a Friday night" (Smith 2003, 31). Neither, Monica writes, does she want to cross over to a kind of "buddy-buddy" relationship. And while she recognizes Smith's choice of strategic conceal-ment as a valid one, Monica determines that "there are many ways to establish authority dynamics within the classroom." For her—at least that particular semester, with those particular stu-dents—it meant making her politics of location as a creative writer, MA student, *and* a disabled person a complex text that might facilitate students revisionary thinking about author-ity, disability, and agency. It might, that is, disrupt ideas about what it means to belong in a university setting—for both teach-ers and students.

While the constitutive forces of neoliberalism would have subjects reject elements of the self that presumably interfere with notions of autonomy and self-sufficiency, a feminist repur-posing of agency finds possibility in just this territory. By turning over the smooth terrain of familiar value systems, groundwork is cultivated for new kinds of growth and exploration. This is visible, for instance, in Dae-Joong (D. J.) Kim's (2011) grap-pling with politics of location and pedagogy as determined by his location in a Korean versus a U.S. classroom. As a first time teacher in Korea, he experienced what he describes as "unex-pected authority," that is, authority granted without question because of his ability to readily fit into the expected role of teacher. He was aware that this authority was not earned, but represented an easy match between his subjectivity and cultural expectations—there was little need to assimilate in order to belong. Privileged positions, Rowe argues, secure their power through seeming "universality" and by occluding the social pro-cesses through which privilege is maintained (Rowe 2005, 29). While she addresses white privilege, here D. J. was concerned with the given hierarchal relationship between teacher and student in Korea. Consequently, rather than submitting to an insider status, he sought to create an atmosphere in which both teacher and students were positioned as learners.

When he changed geographic locations, moving to teach university composition in Lincoln, Nebraska, as a nonnative speaker, he no longer fit expectations of an authority. He describes experiencing a mix of both "hospitality and hostility" from the students as they "read" his identity on the first day of class. "Most of them did not recognize me as a teacher; rather, they thought of me as an international student who came in the wrong room," he writes (3). He goes on to consider his transnational identity: "I am a signifier that deconstructs homogeneous national identity in the class. On a geopolitical level, I represented a borderland between American and Asia across the Pacific. On a linguistic level, my articulation with accented English and minor grammatical mistakes undermined my authority as an English teacher."

Ultimately, D. J. decided to make this liminal position as a teacher of English and learner of English visible to his students by addressing the multiplicity of his position: Asian, nonnative speaker, graduate student of contemporary American fiction, and a "visa-holding non-immigrant who can easily be misunderstood as illegal yellow peril." By highlighting these locations, D. J. shows students how our modes of belonging are multiple, contradictory, and fluid. He is both an English-language learner and an advanced graduate student in American fiction; he is both an authority in English (as indicated by his position as instructor) and someone who speaks English with an Asian accent and makes occasional grammatical mistakes (as do most of us, native speakers or not). These (seeming) contradictions break the repetition of what and whom counts as expertise in English, an authoritative teacher, a member of the campus community—and in so doing, they allow us to consider what Rowe calls "the often overlooked conditions of belonging" (Rowe 2005, 28). They prompt us to ask: to what "regulatory practices" must one submit in order to establish oneself as an insider? (29). And for whom are those regulatory practices more rigid? Who carries the greatest burden of disciplining oneself in the name of belonging?

For a course on rhetoric and argument, the modes of belonging that D. J. navigates raise compelling questions about linguistic difference, power, and inclusion. This is particularly important in our local university context, where international students are heavily recruited as tuition-paying customers and, while hospitality exists, so too does hostility. By illuminating his complex location—and making it a point of dialogue with his students—D. J. refuses the repetition of single, fixed readings of his subjectivity. He describes his choice as also opening conversation with his students, as they asked questions about his life and experience in Korea and conflicts between North and South Korea. As he wrote, "Marking my 'situatedness' . . . thawed out frozen borderlands between the students and me" and, in turn, helped him complicate the notion that any teacher holds a finished expertise, including, he jokes, the seemingly "know-it-all native-speaker teacher." Interestingly, new TAs, native speaking or not, often articulate a dread of their students' discovery that they are not know-it-all experts; it is also challenging this idea that often allows for connection and dialogue to occur.

Even as Monica and D. J. found agency in highlighting aspects of their social locations, the purpose of located agency is not to prompt teachers to "come out" about some aspect of their identities. Rather, it is to undertake a process, as do Monica and D. J., of reexamining traditional notions of authority and practices of belonging, locating alternate possibilities, and making rhetorically based decisions—or formulated choices (Maitra 2013)—about how to deploy one's agency. Sometimes, in fact, complicating dualistic assumptions about identity formation means not claiming a (final) location, which I consider in the next section.

REPURPOSING AMBIGUITY AS AGENCY

As Michelle Gibson, Martha Marinara, and Deborah Meem observe in their article "Bi, Butch, and Bar Dyke: Pedagogical Performances of Class, Gender, and Sexuality," scholars interested in challenging cultural norms and essential identities often view the sharing of particular experiences and locations as a crucial means to disrupt prohibitive "universalisms." But the particulars, they write, "have their own universalisms" (Gibson, Marinara, and Meem 2000, 72). That is, if an instructor comes out as a lesbian, students may believe they already know the story of that identity, which is based largely on what it is not—straight. For this reason, the authors advocate a move away from viewing locations as grounded, which "negates the possibility for inter-reference between any two [or more] landscapes" (73). Instead, they call for highlighting the fluid ways we enact our identities depending on the ever-shifting relationships we negotiate.

One of my students, Sindu Sathiyaseelan, navigates this very territory in her essay, "Negotiating the Bi-nary: Strategic Ambiguity and the Non-nameable Identity in the Classroom." As a bisexual female—one who wears "shoulder-length hair" and has an "affinity for pencil skirts"—she is aware that her students are likely to read her as straight (Sathiyaseelan 2011, 3). Her concern is both with remaining "in the closet" in the classroom and with foreclosing an opportunity for her students—especially those who identify as GLBTQ—to work with an "out" teacher. She is also aware of the tensions between enacting her identity as a campus activist for GLBTQ issues and as a classroom instructor in a red state: what are her roles and responsibilities in each site? And yet she understands that the narrative of "coming out" often boxes subjects in to identity categories that are based on "hegemonic ideals of normative behavior" (2). As someone who is "not gay or lesbian but rather something beyond the binary itself," (3) coming out is not as simple as identifying herself as occupying one side of a dualism.

Sindu draws from Marinara, who, in the aforementioned article, describes performing her identity as bisexual in the classroom, moving in and out of positions of straight and lesbian. Bisexuality, Marinara argues, cannot be easily pinned down as a knowable social category, and consequently, it is an "identity without visible rules, almost without referent" (Gibson, Marinara, and Meem 2000, 73). This allows Marinara to strategically deploy her locations in a way that "poses hard questions about the nature and definitions of political subject positions" (75). She also observes the alliance with and responsibility to queer students resulting from her named location. When she and her students encounter a text with a gender-ambiguous narrator who describes physically intimate relations with a man, her first instinct is to dodge questions of sexuality. The weight of stares from three lesbian students, however, nudges her to examine same-sex affection as part of their collective reading.

Marinara's enactment of an identity that is multiple and fluid allows Sindu to enact a located agency not by verbally claiming her identities but by performing ambiguity. She writes, "However important my coming out may be to me, it is perhaps reinforcing binaries to label myself in any way in the classroom. Instead, I seek to complicate my students' understandings of gender and sexuality by performing a non-nameable ambiguity." While she considers that this choice may reinforce notions of neutrality, she differentiates it from a neutrality that functions in opposition to a "politicized" identity. Rather, it involves "stepping in and out of my queerness" in a way that demonstrates a "constantly shifting identity that resists categorization and dichotomization" (Sathiyaseelan 2011, 4). Sindu holds that this allows her a "strategic positionality" that facilitates an ability to question students' resistance to (or easy embracing of) particular texts without it being read as her personal response; at the same time, it also allows her to ally herself, when this is called for, with queer students. In this way, Sindu repurposes ideas of neutrality or ambiguity, showing how these locations can be engaged to challenge, rather than affirm, fixed identity categories.

At the same time, this complication of dualistic, fixed categories of identity also serves as a useful reminder about how we read students. As the teachers I work with consider their own social locations in relation to their students, they are often surprised at the complexity of their students' positions and locations. They learn that teaching in a "red state," working with rural students, or even engaging with a particular learning community does not mean a uniformity of positions, assumptions, or locations. Located agency should, ideally, make room for both teachers and students to approach identity more expansively and as in process—and, as I argue in the next section, allow for connections among subjects to be made.

AGENCY AS ALLIANCE

While neoliberal agency valorizes individualism, the subject who acts alone in service of individual gain and efficacy, located agency ultimately involves a turn toward others. For Rowe, this means a rewriting of "I-dentity" to a sense of "self" that is "radically inclined toward others, toward the communities to which we belong, with whom we long to be, and to whom feel accountable" (Rowe 2005, 18). This shift repurposes agency from "power over" to "power with." When I'm working with new teachers, this distinction often arises as we discuss grading. Initially, new teachers may view the institutional requirement of grading as evidence that they (must) hold power over their students; they *are* authorities in this regard. While examining the power dynamics that are constituted by grading practices is important—indeed, they are the determiners of their students' grades—I also prompt them to consider how grading is enacted, and what choices are available in this enactment. As one of my teaching mentors framed the questions, "How do you want to use grades? What values do you want the grading, as part of your pedagogy, to promote?" How, then, might grading function to enact power with students?

Enacting a located agency serves both as a vehicle for making the university a more hospitable place for the individual subject and as a means to make connections with others. As Rich emphasized in her articulation of politics of location, the aim is not simply to articulate the self but to reflect on one's responsibility to others as a result of one's location, to ask how connections and alliances can be created as a consequence of this articulation. I often share with new TAs my effort, during my first pregnancy, to deny the reality of my changing body—to deny, really, my body entirely. This choice was in part tied to local conditions: it was my first year as a tenure-line faculty member, teaching in a traditional program that relied, in many ways, on traditional hierarchies. I was the first tenure-line woman in the department to have a baby. My pregnant body felt like a clear marker that I didn't belong, that I wasn't properly occupying the role of (disembodied) intellectual who held expertise and authority over her students.

At the same time, I certainly didn't see myself as formulating a choice. I was simply abiding by normative modes of belonging; to belong, I would need to downplay this aspect of myself that didn't fit dominant conceptions of "the professor." As someone committed to critical and feminist pedagogies, I would normally have critiqued this position, but as my physicality changed, the pressure of the normative model seemed to foreclose other possibilities. As LeCourt and Napoleone write, "Much like whiteness, the 'normal' academic body is a transparent signifier that is visible only when it is contrasted with what it is 'not'" (LeCourt and Napoleone 2011, 86). And this "normal academic body" was clearly not (I feared) a woman with a swelling body, waves of dizziness, and back pain. Consequently, I hid my belly behind the teacher's desk, wore loose clothing, and covered my pregnancy with silence.

With time, more experience, and more conversation with women, I began to see not only how choosing to downplay this experience felt burdensome to me, but also that it foreclosed possibilities for the very kinds of connections and alliances I craved. LeCourt describes a similar experience in trying to cover her working-class identity, noting that such fears become internalized and experienced as an individual problem, demarcating one's own (in)ability to "be an academic" (LeCourt and Napoleone 2011, 95). She notes that it took her a long time to think about how performing marginalized aspects of her identity could be understood as an act of agency, so that "what I had seen as inappropriate slips could actually be something I used more consciously" (99). Like LeCourt, it took me time and experience before I risked challenging hegemonic belonging;

this came partly as a result of moving toward tenure and becoming more familiar with my institutional context, but it was also facilitated by the understanding that performing parts of my identity that fall outside of "the normal academic" not only created opportunities for cultural disruption of categories like "expertise" and "authority" and "intellect" but also opened avenues for connection and alliance with others. In subsequent semesters, graduate students and other female faculty members approached me, for instance, about navigating professional and parenting demands; I also found it important to advocate for space for lactation rooms and to change maternity leave policies that made it difficult to "belong" during my first pregnancy and childbirth experience.

We see examples of enacting "power with" in the narratives above as well. For instance, when Sindu finds ways to illuminate her queer identity so that she can serve as an ally to GLBTQ students, she exercises "power with." When Monica acknowledges to her students that she will sometimes need to ask for help reaching the screen, she demonstrates an authority that also requires relationship with and reliance on others. This parallels the way we hope our students will find ways to write with agency in their writing at the same time that they will come to understand writing as a collaborative process that is aided by the input of others. When D. J. presents himself as a language learner, he disrupts the ideas that the teacher is a finished product and that learning language is ever complete. He and his students are learners together.

Of course, as is true of all pedagogical practices—and contrary to what standardized educational models promote—there is no guaranteed outcome; there is no promise that students will embrace or learn from a "power with" approach. Some students will inevitably crave a traditional classroom dynamic or a teacher who performs agency in ways that are expected and familiar. Brueggemann describes receiving a paper from a student who wrote, "My mother doesn't think it's right that my English teacher is deaf" (Brueggemann and Moddelmog 2003, 214). And yet comments like this only underscore the need

to disrupt the cultural repetition of assumptions and stereo-
types; they make the work of challenging norms of able-ism and
modes of belonging all the more crucial.

Enacting a located agency requires a different kind of risk
than does abiding by normative expectations. Students may
become uncomfortable or hostile; the teacher may become
uncomfortable or fear (or experience) a deeper sense unbe-
longing in the classroom. Even so, as Brueggemann and
Moddelmog argue, the "risk of discomfort" can coexist with the
"concurrent possibility of discovery" (2003, 216) and, I would
add, the concurrent possibility of alliance and connection. I
have noticed that when TAs talk about enacting different modes
of agency and belonging in their classes, it creates opportunities for others to do the same. They develop connections among
themselves and find ways to support each other through the risk
taking. Indeed, as the conversation I opened this chapter with
ensued, the male TA reflected that his students could not see
the background of poverty in which he grew up or the fact that
his family had for a time been homeless. But what if they could?
he asked. How would knowing I didn't come from the middle
class change my students' assumptions about a college instructor? About belonging in this institution?

As we learn from each other's locations and belongings, we
can begin to cross lines of separation that "deaden and wound"
(Rowe 2005, 38). Indeed, part of working with new students—
whether they are first-year writers or graduate students—is
acknowledging the complexity of belonging and fostering
opportunities to facilitate practices that support inclusivity and
connection. A located agency, then, is a process that aims to
value knowledge produced from our embodied locations and
to insist on education as relational, served by connection with
and responsibility to others. It refuses notions of standardized
transactions and insists upon reflexivity regarding our own subjectivities and the contexts in which we live and work. In the last
chapter, I expand upon the issue of educational responsibility,
showing how feminist thought helps to repurpose notions of
neoliberal responsibility as accountability (often to externally

imposed standards) to a responsibility to our students, our colleagues, and our communities.

NOTE

1. The collection *The Teacher's Body: Embodiment, Authority, and Identity in the Academy* (Freedman and Holmes 2003), for instance, traces teachers' navigation of disability, pregnancy, race, sexual orientation, size, age, and linguistic difference in the classroom.

5

REPURPOSING RESPONSIBILITY
From Accounting to Responding Well

FOUR SNAPSHOTS FROM THE
ACCOUNTABILITY MOVEMENT

In a January 2013 radio interview, Governor Pat McCrory of North Carolina promised to forward legislation that would base state funding for public colleges and universities on post-graduation employment rather than enrollment. Or as he put it, "It's not based on butts in seats but on how many of those butts can get jobs" (Kiley 2013). The governor also questioned the value of public funding for liberal arts education, and when radio host Bill Bennett joked about gender courses at UNC–Chapel Hill, McCrory responded, "If you want to take gender studies that's fine, go to a private school and take it. But I don't want to subsidize that if that's not going to get someone a job."

***

In August 2013, Barack Obama spoke of the need to make college education more affordable. As part of his message about increasing access to college, he outlined a plan to "pay colleges and students for performance." To identify colleges that provide the "best value" and to encourage college improvement, Obama announced that the Department of Education will develop and publish a new college ratings system by 2015. As part of reauthorizing the Higher Education Act, the president will support legislation that allocates financial aid based on these ratings, which will evaluate access (such as percentage of Pell grants), affordability (average tuition, scholarships, loan debt), and outcomes, including graduation rates, advanced degrees granted, and graduate earnings (White House 2013).

***

In my e-mail inbox this morning was a message to the faculty from my university's chancellor. He explained that increasingly, "universities are being held accountable for the career success of their recent gradu-

DOI: 10.7330/9781607323884.c005

ates"—as was reflected in Obama's aforementioned speech. In answer to these calls for accountability, he announced his decision to move the reporting relation of the university's Career Service Office to Academic Affairs. He writes, "If the academic colleges are going to be held accountable, they should have a more direct responsibility and engagement with this program."

***

In my postal mailbox this afternoon, I found a letter from my daughter's middle school that contained her "Nebraska Sate Accountability Individual Student Report." These tests, the letter said, are "intended to measure, report and compare student performance on academic content standards in all Nebraska public school buildings." When she got home, I asked her how the test related to what she learned in school. "It covers the bare bones," she answered.

***

I highlight these snapshots not because they are unusual but because they capture a cultural repetition of what has become a commonsense approach to education. They point to dominant understandings of the purpose of education (to prepare a future workforce), through what means that preparation occurs (standardized curricula), and how the outcomes of education are measured (standardized tests and job placement). This view of education, which is deeply entrenched in neoliberalism, is articulated most clearly in conversations about accountability, which in turn shape cultural beliefs about to whom, and to what, education is responsible.

Kristie Fleckenstein argues that the "taken-for-granted worldview" of the accountability movement is Cartesian perspectivalism—a perception and an epistemology defined by disembodied rationality, quantification, and linear causality (Fleckenstein 2008, 86). For instance, cultural discourse on education takes for granted that accountability is tethered to neoliberal accounting—demonstrating, as Chris Gallagher puts it, to those who "pay the bills" that the school or university is a "good investment" by "performing well in a competitive market" (Gallagher 2007, 6–7). Within this framework, educators are primarily responsible to, and checked by, the health of the economy. Drawing from the work of political scientist Andreas Schedler, Linda Adler-Kassner and Susanmarie Harrington observe that accountability is most commonly "associated with the idea of keeping power in check" (qtd. in Adler-Kassner and Harrington 2010, 84). In the contemporary scene of education, this results in a dynamic whereby educators are made answerable, first and foremost, to employers and the economy.

This model of accountability, then, necessarily relies on a guilt/blame logic; if our economy is stalling or America is falling behind in the global marketplace, someone must be to blame. That "someone" in this formula is usually schools, universities, and teachers. Those of us in composition and rhetoric are all too familiar with this logic, since literacy instruction has historically served as a public target of rebuke. To offer but one recent example, the highly publicized critique of contemporary university education *Academically Adrift: Limited Learning on College Campuses* opens with former Harvard president Derek Bok's complaint that "most students" graduate from college "without being able to write well enough to satisfy their employers'" (quoted in Arum and Roksa 2011, 1). Writing instructors, the message goes, are not properly answering employers' needs. They are not upholding their responsibility to the economy or, it might be said, they are not demonstrating adequate compliance, which becomes a synonym for responsibility within an accountability logic.

I want to be clear that the problem with this logic is not the desire to help our students discover and pursue satisfying careers. I imagine that all faculty members share in the hope that their students find themselves engaged in meaningful employment when they graduate from college. My concern is rather with the firmly entrenched notion that accountability is, seemingly *must be*, linked strictly to economic ends. I agree with Gallagher that the problem of accountability is that it asks *too little* of our schools and universities (Gallagher 2007, 18). It addresses, as my daughter says, only the "bare bones" of learning. Narrowing the scope of education to neoliberal accountability forecloses more expansive purposes for education and limits conceptions of to whom and to what postsecondary education is responsible.

While neoliberal approaches to accountability house responsibility within the framework of "answerability"—often to the point that they become interchangeable terms—my aim in this chapter is to distill understandings of responsibility from this neoliberal framework, and in this way, to repurpose educational responsibility. Philosopher Annika Thiem, drawing from Judith Butler, argues that when responsibility is no longer based in accountability—as a response to norms and rules—we can view it more productively as a question that "arises out of relations to others," always in specific historical and cultural contexts, of "how to respond well" (Thiem 2008, 5). She writes, "We become responsible not because actions can be attributed to us and we can be held accountable for them but because we are addressed by others in ways that demand we respond, and respond well" (145). No longer framed in a guilt/blame logic, repurposed responsibility requires us to consider who is addressing us, or to whom we are responsible, and how we can best respond in each particular moment. Adler-Kassner and Harrington also call for separating responsibility from accountability. Within the responsibility framework they articulate, teachers are agents, not objects, of educational processes. Teachers enact responsibility by asking and answering key questions, such as "To whom are we responsible? For what? What voices need to be heard? And how do we act on our understandings of these responsibilities?" (Adler-Kassner and Harrington 2010, 90).

Building on Adler-Kassner and Harrington's and Thiem's frameworks, this chapter calls for a repurposed responsibility that both severs the naturalized link between education and neoliberal accountability and makes room for the feminist values, knowledges, and practices I've forwarded in the prior chapters: situated, reflexive knowledge; careful listening and genuine dialogue; and acknowledgment of learning as complex and affective. I argue that responding well as educators—being responsible—means taking into account multiple views, with special attention to teachers' perspectives; engaging in dialogue and listening; and embracing the complexity of teaching and learning. This chapter, then, invites a consideration of how we might think differently about education, and in particular about writing instruction and assessment, when we foreground responsibility over accountability.

EDUCATING FOR THE MARKET; WRITING FOR THE MARKET

Because educational accountability is deemed common sense, questions of to whom, to what, and how universities must be responsible often go unasked. As a result, the appropriate expectations for and outcomes of education are assumed instead of discussed. For instance, in a recent *Inside Higher Ed* article on public university accountability, former education secretary Margaret Spellings argues that the goal of accountability is to establish "tools and metrics, multiple or otherwise, that are comprehensible and actionable for consumers and policy makers . . . to reassure them that institutions are doing what we need them to be doing" (quoted in Lederman 2013). Here, universities and colleges answer to consumers (those who pay taxes and tuition) and policy makers by way of quantifiable, measurable outcomes. The vague description of education's purpose— "doing what we need them to be doing"—implies a need so naturalized it need not be articulated.

Her words, of course, echo the sentiment articulated in the 2006 Spellings Commission Report, which represented a key public effort to extend the accountability agenda of No Child Left Behind to postsecondary education. The report, as Gallagher observes, "reads as a primer on neoliberal education discourse" (Gallagher 2011, 454). While this report has been thoroughly treated elsewhere (see Gallagher 2007; 2011; Green 2009; Huot 2002), I revisit its values and logics for how they illuminate the habitual neoliberal norms of the larger accountability movement.

The impetus for the report is the failure of U.S. postsecondary institutions to keep up with global competitors; they are not, the report claims, doing their job in ensuring the economic security of individual citizens and the country as a whole. While the report calls for accountability to the "public good," it's clear that this "good" is economic. The commission describes a world that is "becoming tougher, more competitive, less forgiving of wasted resources and squandered opportunities." Our nation's wealth, the report argues, is dependent on educating citizens "who are to able to work smarter and learn faster" (Commission on the Future of Higher Education 2006, ix). Achieving this goal is not possible, the commission contends, unless universities demonstrate accountability to the economy's demands.

While the view of education informing this report is clearly shaped by neoliberalism (the commission includes executives from IBM, Kaplan, Inc., Microsoft, and Educap, Inc.), Fleckenstein aptly argues that it *functions* as Cartesian perspectivalism; that is, it assumes a rational, objective logic that presents itself as a "view from everywhere" (Fleckenstein 2008, 98). While this view claims to see everything, the lens and location of the viewer is obscured—disembodied and detached from any particular context, perspective, or situation. This reveals the larger power dynamic at play: Cartesian perspectivalism relies on a clear dichotomy between an empowered seer and the disempowered seen (92). Intervening in the dominant view, then, requires attention to how the "seer" is situated.

Fleckenstein locates this view by bringing into focus the "elective affinities," or the close alliances, of Cartesian perspectivalism: capitalism and science. These affinities are the "cultural phenomena" that gravitate around it to "reinforce, enact, and disseminate its view of reality" (Fleckenstein 2008, 93). Within the Spellings Report—as well as the wider conversation about education reform—higher education is diagnosed as a failed business (94) and prescribed market-based remedies like "quality assurance," benchmarks or, as we see in the K–12 context, "evidence-based" practices and pedagogies. What constitutes "evidence" depends on a narrow view of science that relies on a seemingly "objective" observation—a view from everywhere—of that which can be controlled, quantified, and compared for the sake of competition. The No Child Left Behind Act, for instance, draws clear lines around what counts as "scientifically based" research: it must involve the "application of rigorous, systematic, and objective procedures to obtain reliable and valid knowledge" (quoted in Gallagher 2007, 123). Similarly, the federally funded research database on education includes only studies that rely on experiments conducted under randomized control conditions. While such methodology might serve disciplines like agriculture, medicine, and the hard sciences, Fleckenstein notes that these parameters render invisible research that examines literacy as a complex, context-specific process (Fleckenstein 2008, 97). Furthermore, in the name of an "objective" view, teachers' perspectives, observations, and judgments—which emerge from their located, relational work with students—are hidden from sight.

In addition to its affiliation to science and capitalism, Cartesian perspectivalism is also steeped in paternalism—infantilizing and feminizing teachers and, often, students. In this framework, the seer is a masculine, unmarked, or disembodied subject who scrutinizes a feminized object/body. That which is feminized is deemed wrong—in need of discipline. This is not a dynamic new to the accountability movement, certainly, nor is it merely metaphorical. In her historical analysis of public discourse on education, Margaret J. Marshall traces the emergence of the now-familiar belief that "individual teachers rather than economic conditions or institutional structures are to blame for the failings of schools" to the early 1800s. The answer then was to provide teachers with programs of professionalization that instilled the values of the elite (Marshall 2004, 37). These teachers, by the end of the nineteenth century, were largely women, as men increasingly occupied supervisory roles over them (46). This is not so different from our contemporary educational culture, in which teachers remain culturally feminized and must answer to the "stern father morality" (Gallagher 2007, 29) dictated by policy makers, administrators, and employers. It's a dynamic that denies teacher agency and expertise, since teachers are rendered mere deliverers of curriculum- and evidence-based practices not developed by them. Even more, they are made responsible to measures and educational purposes they did not have a hand in articulating.

When viewed through Cartesian perspectivalism, being responsible means submitting to the gaze of *assurance* mechanisms, which are also informed by neoliberalism, objectivism, and paternalism. Though often conflated, assurance measures are distinct from assessment which, at least ideally, focuses on *improving* teaching and learning. Assurance measures, in contrast, are designed to *prove* to the public that the institution is doing its job, increasingly through standardized tests—delivered by private vendors—that enable comparison and competition among universities (Adler-Kassner and Harrington 2010, 80–81). Driven by neoliberal pressures, these assurance mechanisms make transparent to consumers how well the university is competing in the global marketplace as well as against its fellow institutions. One such example is the Voluntary System of Accountability (2014) (VSA), which emerged as a preemptive measure to the mandate they feared coming after the Spellings Report. According to the VSA's website, it aims to "assemble and disseminate information that is transparent, comparable and understandable." While "transparency" implies a clear view into the workings of the university, the VSA offers a very particular view—which becomes *the* view—designed to allow for consumer choice based on standardized measures.

The VSA aims to show the "value added" of a degree based on standardized tests, the Collegiate Assessment of Academic Proficiency exam (CAAP), and Collegiate Learning Assessment (CLA). The degree of "value" is measured when universities issue a standardized test in the first and senior years of students' college careers, though not always to the same cohort of students. In terms of its assessment of writing, both the CLA and CAAP rely on timed essays. The CLA features prompts designed to mimic "work samples" that students "might face in the 'real world'" (Hersh n.d., 1). These are not measures designed by instructors, nor do they measure the teaching and learning engaged in the institution. Rather, they are designed to assure the public that the institution is accountable for the success of externally imposed purposes of education. The problem, as Fleckenstein correctly argues, is that in the view of Cartesian perspectivalism, what is measured becomes what is valued; if it can't be measured, it's not considered valuable (2008, 103). This results in an extremely narrow view of writing and learning.

This is not to say, however, that the Cartesian view has gone uncontested, or that its disruption is impossible. Encouragingly, as of spring 2013, the VSA decided to allow institutions to substitute standardized tests with American Association of American Colleges and University's (AACU) VALUE rubrics, which are developed by teams of educators based on disciplinary practices, in order to measure critical thinking or written communication. This change came as a response to university opposition to the VSA's strict reliance on standardized measures. According to *Inside Higher Ed*, about two-thirds of approximately 500 members of the Association of Public and Land Grant Universities and the American Association of State Colleges and Universities participated in the VSA, and of those, only half reported scores using the approved standardized tests (Lederman 2013).

Even so, there are notable limits to the VSA's compromise, pointing to assumptions and values that require ongoing scrutiny. VSA officials refused, for instance, to include locally developed assessment processes as sanctioned measures of "value added." Executive director of VSA Christine Keller explains that the purpose of the system is to provide comparison or benchmarking, and locally developed assessment does not allow for this. She further notes, "I don't buy the argument that you can't use outcomes measures for institutional accountability and for internal purposes" (quoted in Lederman 2013). In other words, she views assurance measures and the seemingly "objective" view they provide as equally amenable to improvement of teaching and learning. The "view from everywhere" is understood to offer an all-encompassing perspective on teaching and learning. As such, the gaze of accountability appears to be detached from particular values and agendas, when in fact its lens is sharply focused on neoliberal processes and products.

When lodged inside the accountability framework, teaching and learning are always responsible to an economic gaze; they remain in a defensive position of seeking to measure up or provide assurance. For this reason, feminist scholars argue for repurposing responsibility by removing it from the purview of accountability (Adler-Kassner and Harrington 2010; Butler 1988; Thiem 2008). As Adler-Kassner and Harrington argue, developing an alternative stance toward education requires a reframing of the stories we tell about teaching, learning, writing, and assessment based on what we want, not what we *don't* want (Adler-Kassner and Harrington 2010, 86). They encourage us to think toward a responsibility frame that is defined by acting from our own commitments, rather than reacting to the accountability agenda. In the next section, I argue that this process begins by interrupting the view from everywhere with the located views of educators.

FEMINIST RESPONSIBILITY: A VIEW FROM SOMEWHERE

Feminist objectivity means quite simply situated knowledges.
—Donna Haraway

As I have argued throughout his book, feminist repurposing begins with illuminating as value laden and situated that which has been deemed natural or "objective." In this case, moving toward a repurposed responsibility means highlighting the location of the accountability "view from everywhere" as situated within neoliberalism, narrow conceptions of scientific objectivism, and paternalism. Considering the partiality of all views is, in fact, what allows for genuine dialogue about the purpose of education, and to whom, and what, it should be responsible. As feminist scientist Donna Haraway (1988) argues, it is the *denial* of location—not "bias" or "interest"—that leads to irresponsible knowledge claims.

A responsibility logic, then, rewrites Cartesian perspectivalism—or, as Haraway names it, "the conquering gaze from nowhere"—by insisting on "the embodied nature of all vision" (Haraway 1988, 581). When these embodied views are joined together, they create a spectrum that allows for a fuller examination of our purposes, practices, and responsibilities as well as for the possibility of new views and choices that normative lenses may exclude. To this end, Fleckenstein promotes the "proliferation of multiple ways of seeing" as a corrective to Cartesian perspectivalism (Fleckenstein 2008, 106). A "many-seeing orientation," she argues, allows for the interplay of perspectives that enhance our ability to understand and respond to a problem (110).

Much like the feminist scholars I referenced in chapter 4, feminist scientists like Haraway and Sandra Harding (1991) promote a standpoint epistemology that privileges marginalized perspectives; they not only challenge a "view from everywhere," they also illuminate the epistemological and scientific benefits of views from *somewhere*. Haraway advocates pursuing the perspectives of those who have been excluded from view, or whose sight is deemed "limited," because these standpoints allow for "connections and unexpected openings" in our knowledge practices (Haraway 1988, 590).

A feminist responsibility model for education, then, abides by this notion that all views are situated and embodied, and that responsibility is relational—it requires dialogue and negotiation among views, with special attention to those who have the most direct view of the scene of education (and yet who are most often excluded from these conversations): teachers and learners. It is these perspectives that help us to approach responsibility not as compliance to norms but as a dialogue about educational aims, purposes, and processes.

Composition scholars, of course, have made strong and effective calls for assessment processes that feature local and located views—practices that view the teaching and learning of writing as necessarily situated. As Gallagher (2014) argues in his *CCC* review essay "All Writing Assessment Is Local," which examines four recently published books on assessment, local has been one of our field's "watchwords" since Brian Huot (1996) published his essay "Toward a New Theory of Writing Assessment." Huot established five oft-cited principles for writing assessment:

site based, locally controlled, context sensitive, rhetorically based, and accessible (562). Like feminist scholars who insist that responsible epistemology acknowledges its location, composition assessment scholars maintain that responsible assessment practices are developed from the site of teaching and learning, are driven by teachers' questions, and result in information that enhances, or sponsors the revision of, teaching and learning (Adler-Kassner and Harrington 2010; Broad 2003; Gallagher 2007, 2011; Huot 1996, 2002).

In fact, Adler-Kassner and Harrington argue that a starting point for a responsibility framework is the "identification of one's interests and values" (2010, 87). This emphasis on *all* assessment practices as situated challenges the normative accountability lens that leaves purposes, audiences, context—and the power dynamics that shape them—unaccounted for. This subsequently results in unarticulated, or uncontested, assumptions about "who holds the power to define and evaluate what students in college should learn, how they should learn what they should, and why" (85). Alternatively, a repurposed responsibility logic insists that universities cannot respond well to these questions unless a range of views is invited, including, most important, those of educators. Instead of assuming that assessment for the purpose of improvement is only for internal audiences, a responsibility logic holds that public audiences benefit from comprehending how teachers and professors are assessing, understanding, and improving their own educational sites. In fact, the visibility of these perspectives is crucial to changing public understandings of education's purposes and practices, not to mention disrupting assumptions about how educational responsibility is enacted.

We find one such effort to highlight teachers' views of education and assessment in Gallagher's *Reclaiming Assessment*, which provides detailed portraits of how K–12 teachers in Nebraska enacted a locally controlled, teacher-led assessment system aimed at school improvement. The School-Based Teacher-Led Assessment and Reporting System (STARS) disrupted the accountability agenda not only by making teacher expertise central to the assessment process but also by emphasizing the importance of local context. The annual State of the Schools Report included information about student performance, assessment quality (the state evaluated the technical quality of each district's assessment mechanism), and student and teacher demographics. As Gallagher notes, "This allows the reader to place school results in context, including how the school is changing from year to year. What it does not allow the reader to do—to the chagrin of some local media—is draw easy comparisons between and among school districts" (Gallagher 2007, 108). While STARS eventually fell victim to the accountability agenda, *Reclaiming Assessment* illuminates a process that enacts responsibility and that can inform assessment discussion from kindergarten to college.[1] Indeed, our colleagues at the K–12 level have more experience navigating—and challenging—neoliberal assessment pressures, and their views are vital to enriching our own.

At the postsecondary level, we see similar efforts to share with the public assessment efforts that are designed to improve education in local settings, not merely to prove compliance. Institutional e-portfolios are one such example: locally generated and context-specific assessment results provide useful information to both internal and external audiences. One of the first of these initiatives, the Urban Universities Portfolio Project, invited six institutions to design e-portfolios that enhanced understanding among internal and external audiences of an institution's "distinguishing features, mission, and goals" (Lorenzo and Ittelson 2005, 2). Here, assessment is built from a university's particular context and goals—not according to externally imposed standards. The project encouraged institutions to use this process on a continual basis for reflection and improvement, even though achieving accreditation was often the initial exigency. Of the six, three universities—Indiana University–Purdue University Indianapolis (IUPUI), Portland State University (PSU), and California State University–Sacramento (CSUS)—continued to develop their e-portfolios. These institutional portfolios allow universities to highlight their programmatic and institutional commitments that shape teaching and learning. They also include multifaceted information like student learning samples, locally developed rubrics, and plans for improvement. In this way, they have the potential to highlight a more expansive array of educational perspectives and purposes and to make public the efforts faculty undertake to study and improve teaching in their local contexts.

Even within the context of the VSA, some institutions that opted out of using or reporting standardized measures instead offer a link to institutional assessment processes. While these may not be sanctioned by the VSA as "value-added" measures, they nevertheless offer richer views of assessment and make visible other lenses for documenting teaching and learning. A responsibility lens, then, not only brings more views of education and assessment processes into focus, it allows for more perspectives—most important, those of teachers—to participate and be seen in the public view of educational discourse.

ENACTING RESPONSIBILITY THROUGH LISTENING AND DIALOGUE

For feminist scholars, a repurposed responsibility is grounded not in compliance (for example, how do I demonstrate that my actions have matched norms?) but in relation to those who address us (for example, how do I hear your call and respond well?) (Thiem 2008). In many ways, this parallels the approach to writing we foreground in composition and rhetoric. In an accountability model, writing is understood as skill based, a-contextual, and measurable according to (seemingly universal) norms. Our field's statements about writing (such as the WPA Outcomes Statement and the Framework for Success in Postsecondary Education) instead emphasize rhetorical awareness and agility that allow a writer to adapt to different audiences, situations, and conventions. The Framework for Success, in fact, highlights the necessary habits of mind for college writers, including responsibility, flexibility, openness, metacognition, and reflexivity. Understood this way, writers need to learn to investigate and participate in the relationships that shape a context (Fleckenstein 2008). To be a responsible writer, teacher, citizen, and employee requires an ability to think with others, to listen rhetorically, and to respond deliberately. Responsibility as relational emphasizes the possibilities that emerge when many views and voices are brought together, rather than when a singular view is imposed.

In the context of assessment, demonstrating responsibility means creating opportunities for dialogue, listening, and fostering alliances across constituencies (Adler-Kassner and Harrington 2010). Because the accountability framework tends to obscure specificity about how we define purposes, audiences, and processes for assessment, it is vital both to bring these rhetorical contingencies into view and to share our perspectives with one another—students, administrators, faculty in other departments, policy makers, parents, and so on. Again, composition and rhetoric scholars offer illustrative examples that suggest ways to generate and enact this dialogue.

Bob Broad's Dynamic Criteria Mapping (DCM) uses "streamlined" qualitative inquiry to allow instructors and administrators to come together to "discover, negotiate, and publicize the rhetorical values they employ when judging students' writing" (Broad 2003, 14). While assessment within an accountability framework would measure student writing against predetermined outcomes, norms, or expectations, DCM invites faculty to begin with a set of writing that features "many kinds of rhetorical successes and failures" in order to articulate for themselves the "full range of values at work in the program." Rather than aiming for agreement about how a text should be judged, the focus is on listening to and understanding how a range of perspectives shapes the way writing is valued (Broad 2003, 129). Once evaluators articulate—through lists, maps, categories, and the like—what they value in student writing, they move on to "high-powered professional discussions regarding how they *should* value that writing" (133). Even then, when agreement is reached, or approximated, DCM is designed to change over time. Within a responsibility framework, engaging the question of "How do we respond well to students?" is ongoing.

While Broad argues that rubrics too often aim to make assessment "quick, simple and agreeable," I contend that we can sponsor opportunities for dialogue and listening even within the constraints of outcome-based assessment. That is, as feminist scholars advocate, we can locate ways to move within and against normative practices and structures. At my own institution, we have adopted an outcomes-based general education curriculum (Achievement Centered Education, or ACE), which requires faculty-developed assessment of their courses that address the outcome. In order to present faculty with a flexible model for assessment, administrators asked a colleague, then composition coordinator, and me, then director of a writing in the disciplines program, to design and pilot a sustainable assessment process for student learning outcome (SLO) 1: written communication. We also sought to create a process that was flexible enough that faculty could adapt it for assessment of other SLOs.

One of our central goals in the ACE 1 pilot was to foster faculty development and dialogue about assessment, so we began our process by forming a committee that would collaborate on both the design and enactment of the model. It was important to us that the nearest stakeholders—the teachers of ACE 1 courses—played a central role in this project, so we included instructors of both English and journalism and mass communication writing courses. We also gathered colleagues (both faculty and administrators) with an expressed commitment to writing instruction across the curriculum. We hoped that by including a range of perspectives about the work of writing, we would come to a richer and more nuanced understanding of our outcome and its assessment—as well as more expansive notions of writing and writing instruction itself.

Because one of our charges was to create a process that might be adaptable to other disciplines, we decided to develop a rubric based on outcome 1.[2] However, we did not assume shared assumptions or values regarding the language of the outcome, so we began by defining, collectively, its relevant key terms. The discussion that led to the definition—arguably as valuable as the definition itself—allowed us a window into the roles of writing and research in one another's disciplines and classrooms, enabling us to think relationally and contextually about our responsibilities as writing instructors. It further helped us to recognize and create more rhetorical possibilities for the range of intellectual work in which students engage.

Another key moment for dialogue emerged several years later, when my collaborator and I were asked to present our process to the Board of Regents, which wanted to learn more about how faculty approached ACE assessment. While we initially viewed this as an "accountability" moment—we were being called to the table to justify our actions—we approached the presentation from a responsibility perspective, explaining the importance of assessment that feeds back into the teaching and learning process. We want, we explained, to assess whether our courses are achieving the outcome but, as important, we want the assessment process to be meaningful to the teaching and learning enacted in our program. In turn, the members of the board were interested to hear how we used information from our assessment process to revise our work with TAs and, ultimately, to create a better learning experience for our students. This experience helped me approach such moments differently—less from a position of defense and more from one of responsibility, whereby one of my tasks as writing program administrator is to make our programmatic and disciplinary values visible. Indeed, this is what it means to "claim a public voice" for assessment (Adler-Kassner and Harrington 2010, 94), emphasizing its purpose to improve teaching and learning by foregrounding the question "How do we respond well to students and teachers?"

Zawacki et al. offer another example of promoting dialogue, theirs in the face of a mandate by the state of Virginia to conduct value-added assessment. In their article "Voices at the Table," Terry Myers Zawacki, director of the writing across the curriculum program; E. Shelley Reid, director of composition; Ying Zhou, director of institutional assessment; and Sarah E. Baker, assistant director of writing across the curriculum/ assessment specialist of George Mason University detail how they answered this call while also preserving their commitment (already enacted in their writing across the curriculum program) to assessment designed to improve teaching and learning. Zawacki contends that through dialogue and collaboration among different constituents, they were able to avoid a "the writing people vs. the assessment people" dynamic to instead enact a "much richer, more nuanced, multi-vocal approach, with each of our voices coming to the front or receding as we worked through a collaborative process of discovery." This is not to say there weren't roadblocks. For instance, when Baker brought the group's assessment plan to be reviewed by assessment professionals from peer institutions in the state, one reviewer pushed for standardized (rather than teacher-composed) writing prompts. Baker describes the negotiation this way:

> In our response, we acknowledged the reviewers' concerns but argued—successfully, as it turned out—that our plan would be the least intrusive to faculty teaching, and the data we collected would be most useful for the composition program and individual academic programs. We also reiterated the high value our university places on the culture of writing we've created over the decades, with assessment playing a key role in sustaining that culture by enabling . . . conversations about writing. (Zawacki et al. 2009)

Through dialogue and listening, then, they were able to build an assessment model that both answered the mandate and maintained their responsibility to the writing programs' commitments and values. While I offer only a sketch of these efforts (for fuller versions of these processes, see Blankenship, Stenberg, and Wilson 2013; Zawacki et al. 2009), they demonstrate a different kind of repetition based on responsibility for education through dialogue, sometimes even within the context of accountability mandates.

VIEWING LEARNING RESPONSIBLY: REPURPOSING THE EXCESS OF FAILURE, UNCERTAINTY, AND INQUIRY

In an recent NPR interview, author of the book *"I Don't Know": In Praise of Admitting Ignorance (Except When You Shouldn't)* Leah

Hager Cohen (2013) describes a consequence of education in an accountability climate:

> This year's graduating high school class will be the first generation to have grown up entirely under the No Child Left Behind Act, so this is an entire generation of kids that's been raised in an educational environment where there's a premium on knowing the right answer, being able to fill in the correct oval on a test. I worry that we may not be teaching enough the value of experimentation and failure and risk-taking and the process of inquiry.

Indeed, the linear view of education that shapes the accountability movement leaves little room for the missteps, deviation, and failure that genuine learning requires.[3] An accountability logic, after all, builds a narrow path from acquiring particular skills and knowledge to demonstrating that acquisition in standardized tests to, ultimately, producing good employees who support the economy. It also assumes that only a certain kind of knowledge "counts" on that path, as is underscored by Pat McCrory's quotation at the beginning of this chapter. As Fleckenstein notes, while linear causality may help us plot the trajectory of an object falling from a plane at a particular speed and height, it does not work well as a "paradigm for human action because, unlike billiard balls or bombs, human actions can have very unequal reactions" (Fleckenstein 2008, 104). And, as our field's scholarship on writing and learning development attests, learning is never reducible to a single factor or a cause and effect dynamic. To look at education from such a restrictive view is to miss the richness and complexity of learning as well as the possibilities that emerge from those "unequal reactions" or diverge from a linear track. Indeed, as education scholar Diane Senechal argues, "The danger of the accountability movement lies in its insistence on the generic, literal, and flat, its dismissal of the subtlety and particularity of subject matter" (Senechal 2013, 50)—and, I would add, of the human subjects who enact teaching and learning.

In contrast, a responsibility logic holds a view of learning that is expansive enough to make room for experimentation, conflict, and failure. This requires us, as Elizabeth Ellsworth argues, "to be responsible to . . . those 'small, unnoticeable messages' that have not been given space and have not been allowed to grow for reasons having to do with power, history, and desire" (Ellsworth 1996, 140). In order to bring into view—and to respond to—fuller, richer conceptions of teaching and learning, it is vital to illuminate more than what can be measured or quantified. This involves attending to the emotional dimensions of learning, including failure, uncertainty, and frustration, as well as to the complexities of teaching and learning that defy simple categorization.

Perhaps most in need of repurposing is the concept of failure which, of course, is locked in a strict dualism in our culture, signifying the opposite of success in a society that wants only to win. But as Senechal contends, "Unless we fail at our work now and then, we can understand nothing well"; for this reason, educational responsibility means making room for "uncertainty and failure" on the part of students, teachers, and institutions. She acknowledges that this is a difficult claim to convey to policy makers in an accountability climate, because to accept failure is often understood to suggest that it is acceptable to do poorly. However, she argues to the contrary—that to do our work well, to engage teaching, learning, and researching responsibly, we "must imagine and strive for excellence—and fall short of it often" (Senechal 2013, 52).

While this acceptance of failure as part and parcel of—not in opposition to—good educational practice may not fit within the narrow view of Cartesian perspectivalism, those who practice science, teaching, and writing, among many other fields, know otherwise. Scientists learn from failed experiments; writers learn from drafts that fail, in some way, to achieve their aims. When *Edge* magazine posed the question "What scientific concept would improve everybody's cognitive toolkit?" to leading scientists, philosophers, and artists, the editor at large of *Wired* magazine, Kevin Kelly, pointed to failure. "Failure is not something to be avoided but rather something to be cultivated. That's a lesson from science that benefits not only laboratory research, but design, sport, engineering, art, entrepreneurship, and even daily life itself. All creative avenues yield the maximum when failures are embraced" (quoted in Jha 2011). If failure is embraced as part of teaching and learning rather than forbidden and feared, we open avenues for more risk taking and creativity. We also acknowledge that education is far more complex than any standardized test or any single evaluation can measure.

In addition to recognizing failure as occupying an integral part of the creative and intellectual process, attending to the rhetorical situation of failure may serve to illuminate the conditions and values that label it as such. As I argued of shame in chapter 2, when we no longer relegate shame to the individual but instead look at the cultural contexts that give rise to it, we gain an opportunity for cultural analysis and critique. Judith Halberstam, in *The Queer Art of Failure*, makes a parallel case for failure: "From the perspective of feminism, failure has often been a better bet than success. Where feminine success is always measured by male standards, and gender failure often means being relieved of the pressure to measure up to patriarchal ideals, not succeeding at womanhood can offer unexpected pleasures" (Halberstam 2011, 4). For Halberstam, then, failure prompts us to ask: failed according to what, and whose, ideals? And what are the limits of these measures and ideals?

In the case of No Child Left Behind measures, failure led to public criticism about the structure itself; and at this time, all but two states have applied for waivers, and forty-one states have received them. The question remains, however: will failure prompt careful reflection on the structures and contexts that shape education? Will it foster dialogue among teachers, parents, students, and policy makers about the purposes and practices of education? Failure is generative only if it leads to rethinking and movement. A responsibility framework, then, needs not only to accept failure within the flexible bounds of teaching and learning but also to make room for inquiring into it and locating new possibilities for transformation or revision as a result.

This, of course, is why responsible assessment creates a feedback loop to sites of teaching and learning; the aim is not simply to measure and report but to understand, learn, and revise. Likewise, this is the goal of the writing process; we teach students to write multiple drafts because their writing will head in unexpected directions, it will improve in some ways as it regresses in others, but ideally, each iteration will sponsor learning and change. Challenging the accountability climate, then, means casting a different light on notions of failure, both at the level of classroom teaching and in assessment practices, so that we open multiple paths for movement, reflection, and learning.

I don't pretend this is an easy task. Failure, or even the potential for failure, is something we learn to cover or hide. But this creates a stifling climate for learners, so it is vital for those of us who work with developing teachers and writers to create spaces that allow for the richness of our learning processes to be made visible, even when they are complex and messy. We need to create environments, that is, where the dynamic, recursive, and failure-ridden process of learning is deemed acceptable and productive.

We have grappled with this in our department in relation to the reflections we ask teachers, from TA to full professor, to provide alongside their student evaluations. The teacher is asked to provide an assessment of her or his own performance and the class's performance prior to reading the student evaluations and then, upon reading them, to provide an assessment of the students' evaluations. The purpose of the reflective writing—or "blue sheets," as we call them—is to give the teacher an opportunity to reflect on the connections and divergences between one's own experience of the course and how students describe their experiences. They experience might also allow the teacher to reflect on new practices or approaches employed, and to note and respond to trends in student evaluations. In other words, the goal is to theorize and contextualize teaching in a way that the evaluations (a combination of numeric and short-answer questions) may not make visible in isolation.

As the director of the composition program, I both read teacher reflections and talk with TAs about why we use them and what we hope they will allow. Often, I've found, TAs approach them from an accountability lens—seeing them as a moment when they are required to defend their teaching practice against any perceived "failures" in the form of student critiques or complaints. They are, they presume, required to answer to a logic that locates them as a success or a failure, based on perceived norms or expectations. In this context, success is often pinned to the numeric portion of the evaluation. This isn't surprising, given that our evaluation forms show us where our course numbers stand in relation to department medians.

These responses, then, are understandably read as a requirement to "be accountable" to the department median (which the faculty in my department all agree is exceptionally high—a kind of Lake Wobegon effect), even when that hasn't been named as the goal. The accountability logic is ever present. As I work with TAs, I try to underscore that when the committee members read these reflections, we approach teachers not in terms of accountability but of responsibility, for their ability to "respond well" to their teaching. That is, we are not looking for a demonstration of success or a defense of (perceived) failure—which mires teachers in a guilt/blame logic—but for pedagogical reflection, for listening to the student comments, which may include further contextualization, and for ideas about how one will move forward from this course with new insights. The point is not to name the course as a failure or success (though many teachers seem inclined to so), but to approach the class as always both, as a draft that includes many features and moments.

In an effort to emphasize a responsibility approach to the reflections, we decided to include a discussion of them in our new TA Sourcebook. The graduate student associate coordinators who primarily authored this sought out reflections from peers that move out of a success/failure binary to instead engage in a thoughtful dialogue with their course. Our aim was not to present them as models but to break the repetition of a guilt/blame logic and offer examples that may invite new approaches. We also invited the TAs whose reflections we included to talk about the process of reflecting itself. One of these teachers, James Crews, offered this perspective on the process:

The blue sheets . . . help us to pause and reflect, to look at the bigger picture of every class, before simply moving on to the next one . . . When I sat down to write my blue sheets, it felt like extra work. I privately fumed too: Why do *I* have to do this? Why would I ever want to rehash what was one of the most difficult classes I'd ever taught? Once I started writing, though, I saw how success and failure—arbitrary labels, to be sure—are both part of our path as teachers. The lessons learned from teaching this course have now solidified because I was "forced" to sit down and reflect on what went right and what could have gone better. And I have carried that knowledge with me into each subsequent course I've taught.

Indeed, in a culture that values efficiency and makes constant demands on our time, reflection can seem burdensome, but as James articulates, reflection can allow us to see moments experienced as successes *and* failures as rich material for learning. This, after all, is what we hope our students will learn about their writing process. In the examples we include in the Sourcebook, each teacher locates moments that seemed to "work" as well as those that felt more problematic; the commonality is that they use *both* kinds of moments as a resource for learning. In order to repurpose responsibility as a process that embraces that complexity of learning, we need to make visible accounts that disrupt narrow views of education as either succeeding or failing and instead demonstrate the learning that occurs when we see moments of failure or frustration as vital for learning.

The same need is evident in wider-scale assessment processes. As we developed the pilot assessment process for our general education curriculum, my colleague and I emphasized to faculty and administrators the importance of assessment as ongoing, collaborative inquiry. Our conversations with faculty members across the university revealed that many, much like our TAs, regarded this as a compliance or surveillance mechanism. We stressed to the administrators leading this endeavor that faculty needed reassurance that they could share results of pedagogical efforts that failed or fell short. We wanted instructors to have the space to try things that may not work, to view that failure as an opportunity to learn, and to try something else. This, after all, is the purpose of assessment as it is of teaching: to improve learning by paying attention to the results of our pedagogy.

When the university assessment committee designed the reporting template, it included two questions that help facilitate an orientation toward teacher learning. The first question features the faculty question as the impetus for the assessment process: "What was the question of interest that the department/program investigated related to assessment of [the] ACE learning outcome?" After inviting explanation of the assessment process, the reporting template asks faculty to account for how findings were shared with stakeholders and how they will be used to "improve student learning of the ACE learning outcome." Rather than asking faculty to document success or failure, then, the prompts invite an articulation of the feedback loop—how learning from assessment will result in changed practices. The final question features future investigation: "What assessment questions related to the ACE learning outcome would the department/program like to investigate in the future?" This helps to establish that assessment is a responsibility process, not a compliance event. Good assessment leads to new questions and inquiry, and sometimes the process requires adjustment and retooling, especially if it reflects teachers' and students' changing interests and needs.

Of course, it will take time and trust (a great deal of both, most likely) for faculty to represent the complexity of learning—both failure and success—in their assessment reports. This happens through local, relational work between faculty and administrators, among faculty, and between faculty and students. It means breaking the repetition that deems only "successes" worthy of making public, showing instead how we benefit from risk taking, missteps, and traveling unexpected paths.

RESPONDING WELL

While Cartesian perspectivalism claims a view from everywhere, examining its affiliations with neoliberalism locates its view. To see education strictly as a path to economic gain is to occlude many other views and purposes, including engaged citizenship, creativity and innovation, and inquiry for its own sake. Our students will be better prepared for cultural participation—in the workforce, in their communities, in their families—if they are offered an education that invites them to engage multiple, even conflicting, perspectives; if they are encouraged to inquire, explore, fail, and try again; and if they are valued as intellectual, emotional, embodied subjects. These are certainly feminist principles, but they are also the goals of responsible education.

While documents like the Spellings Report insist that education is in crisis, most of us could point to examples of classrooms that allow exactly the kind of learning I uphold in this book. I have witnessed teachers' enactment of responsibility when I visit TAs' classrooms, when I work with Nebraska Writing Project teachers, when I hear my colleagues describe a new assignment they've designed, or when I go to conferences at my children's schools. This is because, even in an accountability model, education is locally enacted; and very often, it is enacted by teachers committed to *responding well* to their students, their institutions, and their communities.

As Gallagher argues, despite the efforts of neoliberal education reformers to "build remote-control systems" for schooling, teachers continue to be the "critical variables" in students' learning. "In other words," he writes, "for all of the effort neoliberal reformers put into conducting end runs around faculty and students, *being there* matters" (Gallagher 2011, 463). Education scholar Linda Darling-Hammond, who has researched schools in all fifty states, confirms this. She observes that even in the context of directives, "what typically happens is much more a process of redefinition or sometimes subversion" (Darling-Hammond 1997, 70). Teachers, then, are already repurposing responsibility—answering to students ahead of accountability mechanisms.

If neoliberal models promote a dynamic that "maintains the corporate fantasy of relation without flesh and encounter without touch" (Feigenbaum 2007, 340), a repurposed responsibility—severed from accountability logic—depends upon relationships between and among embodied, located teaching and learning subjects. The educational aim of a responsibility model reaches beyond a narrow view of students as future workers to see them more expansively as cultural and civic participants, community members, family members, and so on—each with his or her own purposes and interests for learning. When I taught at a Jesuit university, we commonly referred to the educational principle *cura personalis*—care of the whole person. This principle richly intersected with my own feminist values, underscoring that students are more than "minds"; they are also emotional, spiritual, and physical beings. And it is this view of the student as a whole person and this vision of education as a complex, emotional, recursive process that listens to those at its center—teachers and learners—that serve as the fulcrum of responsible education. In turn, responsible education considers its relationship to the needs of the community, which are served by participants who not only contribute to the economy but also think critically, listen well, and participate actively. As educators, even—indeed, especially—under neoliberal pressures, we need to highlight education as a relational process that is always dependent on the learners in the room, that requires reflexivity and revision, and that takes into account multiple purposes for teaching and learning. This is what it means to respond well.

NOTES

1. Even so, the fact that Nebraska remains one of five states to refuse the adoption of the Common Core Standards shows that this commitment to teachers' knowledge has not been entirely thwarted.

2. Representatives from the composition program participated in the composing of outcome 1, ensuring that it reflected a rhetorical-based approach to writing that is espoused in our program.

3. I thank Zach Beare for our many rich conversations about learning and failure, which inform my thinking here.

REFERENCES

ADE Ad Hoc Committee on Staffing. 2008. "Education in the Balance: A Report on the Academic Workforce in English." Modern Language Association and Association of Departments of English, December 10. Accessed June 12, 2014. http://www.mla.org/pdf/workforce_rpt03.pdf.

Adler-Kassner, Linda, and Susanmarie Harrington. 2010. "Responsibility in the Twenty-First Century." *College Composition and Communication* 62(1): 73–99.

Annas, Pamela J. 1985. "Style as Politics: A Feminist Approach to the Teaching of Writing." *College English* 47(4): 360–371. http://dx.doi.org/10.2307/376958.

Anzaldúa, Gloria. 1987. *Borderlands/La frontera.* San Francisco: Aunt Lute Books.

Archer, Louise. 2008. "The New Neoliberal Subjects? Young/er Academics' Constructions of Professional Identity." *Journal of Education Policy* 23(3): 265–285. http://dx.doi.org/10.1080/02680930701754047.

Aristotle. 1944. "Politics." In *Aristotle in 23 Volumes,* vol. 21. Translated by H. Rackham. Cambridge, MA: Harvard University Press. Accessed June 12, 2014. http://www.perseus.tufts.edu/hopper/text?doc=urn:cts:greekLit:tlg0086.tlg035.perseus-eng1:1.1254b.

Arum, Richard, and Josipa Roksa. 2011. *Academically Adrift: Limited Learning on College Campuses.* Chicago: University of Chicago Press.

Ballif, Michelle, and Roxanne Mountford. 2000. "Towards an Ethics of Listening." *JAC* 20(4): 931–942.

Beall, Melissa L., Jennifer Gill-Rosier, Jeanine Tate, and Amy Matten. 2008. "State of the Context: Listening in Education." *International Journal of Listening* 22(2): 123–132. http://dx.doi.org/10.1080/10904010802174826.

Benson, Jane, Nancy Olson, and Jan Rindfleisch. 1987. *The Power of Cloth: Political Quilts, 1845–1986.* San Francisco: DeAnza College.

Bizzell, Patricia, ed. 2002a. "Feminist Historiography in Rhetoric." Special Issue, *Rhetoric Society Quarterly* 32(1). http://dx.doi.org/10.1080/02773940209391218.

Bizzell, Patricia. 2002b. "The Intellectual Work of 'Mixed' Forms of Academic Discourse." In *Alt Dis: Alternative Discourses and the Academy,* edited by Christopher Schroeder, Helen Fox, and Patricia Bizzell, 1–10. Portsmouth, NH: Boynton/Cook.

Blankenship, Erin, Shari Stenberg, and David E. Wilson. 2013. "Developing a Process for Assessing General Education Learning Outcomes across a Multi-College University." In *Changing the Conversation about Higher Education,* edited by Robert J. Thompson Jr., 113–128. New York: Rowman and Littlefield.

Boler, Megan. 1999. *Feeling Power: Emotions and Education.* New York: Routledge.

Booth, Wayne C. 2005. "Symposium: The Limits and Alternatives to Skepticism: A Dialogue." *College English* 67(4): 378–399. http://dx.doi.org/10.2307/30044679.

DOI: 10.7330/9781607323884.c006

Bordo, Susan. 1987. *The Flight to Objectivity: Essays on Cartesianism and Culture.* Albany: State University of New York Press.

Breslau, Karen. 2008. "Hillary Clinton's Emotional Moment." *Newsweek.com,* January 6. Accessed June 16, 2014. http://www.newsweek.com/hillary-clintons -emotional-moment-87141.

Broad, Bob. 2003. *What We Really Value: Beyond Rubrics in Teaching and Assessing Writing.* Logan: Utah State University Press.

Brown, Brené. 2010. *The Power of Vulnerability. TED* video. https://www.ted.com /talks/brene_brown_on_vulnerability. Accessed June 16, 2014.

Brown, Brené. 2012. *Listening to Shame. TED* video. http://www.ted.com/talks /brene_brown_listening_to_shame#t-4227. Accessed June 16, 2014.

Brownell, J. 1994. "Managerial Listening and Career Development in the Hospitality Industry." *International Journal of Listening* 8(1): 31–49. http://dx.doi .org/10.1080/10904018.1994.10499130.

Brueggemann, Brenda Jo, and Debra A. Moddelmog. 2003. "Coming Out Pedagogy: Risking Identity in Language and Literature Classrooms." In Freedman and Holmes 2003, 209–234.

Brulé, Elizabeth. 2004. "Going to Market: Neo-liberalism and the Social Construction of the University Student as an Autonomous Consumer." In *Inside Corporate U: Women in the Academy Speak Out,* edited by Marilee Reimer, 247–264. Toronto: Sumach.

Burnison, Gary. 2010. "Listen, Learn, and then Lead." *Businessweek.com,* October 1. Accessed June 17, 2014. http://www.bloomberg.com/bw/stories /2010-10-01/listen-learn-and-then-leadbusinessweek-business-news-stock -market-and-financial-advice.

Butler, Judith. 1988. "Performative Acts and Gender Constitution: An Essay in Phenomenology in Feminist Theory." *Theatre Journal* 40(4): 519–531. http:// dx.doi.org/10.2307/3207893.

Campbell, Karlyn Kohrs. 1989. *Man Cannot Speak for Her: A Critical Study of Early Feminist Rhetoric.* 2 vols. New York: Greenwood.

Collaborative for Academic, Social and Emotional Learning. n.d. http://www .casel.org/ Accessed. March 25, 2015.

Cixous, Hélène. 2001. "Sorties." In Ritchie and Ronald 2001, 284–290.

Cochran-Smith, Marilyn, and Susan L. Lytle. 2009. *Inquiry as Stance: Practitioner Research for the Next Generation.* New York: Teachers College Press.

Cohen, Leah Hager. 2013. "Interview with NPR Staff." *Morning Edition,* September 18. Accessed June 19, 2014. http://www.npr.org/2013/09/18/223402246/dont -know-just-admit-it.

Collins, Patricia Hill. 1986. "Learning from the Outsider Within: The Sociological Significance of Black Feminist Thought." *Social Problems* 33(6): S14–32. http://dx.doi.org/10.2307/800672.

Commission on the Future of Higher Education. 2006. *A Test of Leadership: Charting the Future of U.S. Higher Education.* U.S. Department of Higher Education. Accessed June 19, 2014. http://www2.ed.gov/about/bdscomm/list/hiedfuture/repor ts/pre-pub-report.pdf.

Connors, Robert J. 1990. "Overwork/Underpay: Labor and Status of Composition Teachers since 1880." *Rhetoric Review* 9(1): 108–126. http://dx.doi.org /10.1080/07350199009388919.

Crowley, Sharon. 1998. *Composition in the University: Historical and Polemical Essays.* Pittsburgh: University of Pittsburgh Press.

CSPAN. 2013. "Clinton Blows Up at GOP Senator during Benghazi Hearing." *CSPAN.org,* January 13. Accessed June 17, 2014. http://www.c-span.org/video /?c4329984/clinton-blows-gop-senator-benghazi-hearing.

Darling-Hammond, Linda. 1997. *The Right to Learn.* San Francisco: Jossey-Bass.

David, Miriam, and Sue Clegg. 2008. "Power, Pedagogy and Personalization in Global Higher Education: The Occlusion of Second-Wave Feminism?" *Discourse (Abingdon)* 29(4): 483–498. http://dx.doi.org/10.1080/015 96300802410201.

Davies, Bronwyn, Jenny Browne, Susanne Gannon, Lekkie Hopkins, Helen McCann, and Monne Whilborg. 2006. "Constituting the Feminist Subject in Poststructuralist Discourse." *Feminism & Psychology* 16(1): 87–103. http:// dx.doi.org/10.1177/0959-353506060825.

de Certeau, Michel. 1984. *The Practice of Everyday Life.* Translated by Steven Rendall. Berkeley: University of California Press.

Ellsworth, Elizabeth. 1996. "Situated Response-Ability to Student Papers." *Theory into Practice* 35(2): 138–143. http://dx.doi.org/10.1080/00405849609543714.

Emig, Janet. 1972. "Open Letter from Janet Emig, Chairwoman, NCTE Committee on the Role and Image of Women." *English Journal* 61 (5): 710.

Enos, Theresa. 1997. "Gender and Publishing Scholarship in Rhetoric and Composition." In *Publishing in Rhetoric and Composition,* edited by Gary Olson and Todd Taylor, 57–74. Albany: State University of New York Press.

Epstein, Reid J. 2014. "A Brief History of Obama's 'Angry' Moments." *The Wall Street Journal,* May 16. Accessed June 17, 2014. http://blogs.wsj.com/washwire /2014/05/16/a-brief-history-of-obamas-angry-moments/.

Feigenbaum, Anna. 2007. "The Teachable Moment: Feminist Pedagogy and the Neoliberal Classroom." *Review of Education, Pedagogy & Cultural Studies* 29(4): 337–349. http://dx.doi.org/10.1080/10714410701291145.

Fell, Margaret. 2001. "From *Womens Speaking Justified, Proved and Allowed by the Scriptures.*" In. Ritchie and Ronald 2001, 66–70.

Fiumara, Gemma Corradi. 1995. *The Other Side of Language: A Philosophy of Listening.* New York: Routledge.

Fleckenstein, Kristie S. 2008. "A Matter of Perspective: Cartesian Perspectivism and the Testing of English Studies." *JAC* 28(1–2): 85–120.

Flynn, Elizabeth. 1988. "Composing as a Woman." *College Composition and Communication* 39(4): 423–435. http://dx.doi.org/10.2307/357697.

Flynn, Jan, Tuula-Riitta Valikoski, and Jennie Grau. 2008. "Listening in the Business Context: Reviewing the State of Research." *International Journal of Listening* 22(2): 141–151. http://dx.doi.org/10.1080/10904010802174800.

Freedman, Diane P., and Martha Stoddard Holmes, eds. 2003. *The Teacher's Body: Embodiment, Authority, and Identity in the Academy.* Albany: State University of New York Press.

Fresh Air. 2013. "For Key and Peele, Biracial Roots Bestow Special Comedic 'Power.'" *NPR.org,* December 13. Accessed June 17, 2014. http://www.npr .org/templates/transcript/transcript.php?storyId=256605611.

Friedow, Alison. 2009. "Writing Our Way In: Revising Scholarly Scripts in Composition." Unpublished MS.

Gallagher, Chris W. 2007. *Reclaiming Assessment: A Better Alternative to the Accountability Agenda*. Portsmouth, NH: Heinemann.

Gallagher, Chris W. 2011. "Being There: (Re)Making the Assessment Scene." *College Composition and Communication* 62(3): 450–476.

Gallagher, Chris W. 2014. "Review Essay: All Writing Assessment Is Local." *College Composition and Communication* 65(3): 486–505.

Gallagher, Chris W. 2016. "Our Trojan Horse: How Compositionists Were Duped into Promoting Competency-Based Education (and Our Own Irrelevance) through Outcomes Assessment and What We Can Do about It Now." In *Composition in the Age of Austerity*, edited by Tony Scott and Nancy Welch. Logan: Utah State University Press. Forthcoming.

Gardner, Howard. 1985. *The Mind's New Science*. New York: Basic Books.

Gere, Anne Ruggles. 1997. *Intimate Practices: Literacy and Cultural Work in U.S. Women's Clubs, 1880–1920s*. Champaign: University of Illinois Press.

Gibson, Michelle, Martha Marinara, and Deborah Meem. 2000. "Bi, Butch, and Bar Dyke: Pedagogical Performance of Class, Gender, and Sexuality." *College Composition and Communication* 52(1): 69–95. http://dx.doi.org/10.2307/358545.

Gilyard, Keith. 1999. *Race, Rhetoric and Composition*. Portsmouth, NH: Heinemann.

Glenn, Cheryl. 1997. *Rhetoric Retold: Regendering the Tradition from Antiquity through the Renaissance*. Carbondale: Southern Illinois University Press.

Goleman, Daniel. 1995. *Emotional Intelligence: Why It Can Matter More Than IQ*. New York: Bantam.

Graff, Gerald, and Cathy Birkenstein. 2006. *They Say/I Say: The Moves That Matter in Academic Writing*. New York: Norton.

Green, Angela K. 2009. "The Politics of Literacy: Countering the Rhetoric of Accountability in the Spellings Report and Beyond." *College Composition and Communication* 61(1): 367–384.

Greer, Betsy. 2007. "Craftivism." In *Encyclopedia of Activism and Social Justice*, edited by Gary L. Anderson and Kathryn G. Herr, 401. Thousand Oaks, CA: Sage. http://dx.doi.org/10.4135/9781412956215.n218.

Halberstam, Judith. 2011. *The Queer Art of Failure*. Durham, NC: Duke University Press. http://dx.doi.org/10.1215/9780822394358.

Haraway, Donna. 1988. "Situated Knowledges: The Science Question in Feminism and the Privilege of Partial Perspective." *Feminist Studies* 14(3): 575–599. http://dx.doi.org/10.2307/3178066.

Harding, Sandra. 1991. *Whose Science? Whose Knowledge? Thinking from Women's Lives*. Ithaca, NY: Cornell University Press.

Harkin, Patricia. 2006. "Excellence Is the Name of the (Ideological) Game." In *Identity Papers: Literacy and Power in Higher Education*, edited by Bronwyn T. Williams, 29–41. Logan: Utah State University Press.

Healy, Patrick. 2008. "Clinton's Message, and Moment, Won the Day." *Nytimes.com.*, January 10. Accessed June 16, 1014. http://www.nytimes.com/2008/01/10/us/politics/10clinton.html?pagewanted=all&_r=0.

Hedges, Elaine. 1972a. "Women in the Colleges: One Year Later." *College English* 34(1): 1–5. http://dx.doi.org/10.2307/375213.

Hedges, Elaine, ed. 1972b. "Women, Writing and Teaching." Special issue, *College English* 3 (1).

Heidegger, Martin. 1975. *Early Greek Thinking*. Translated by David Farrell Krell and Frank A. Capuzzi. New York: Harper and Row.

Heinrichs, Jay. 2008. *Thank You for Arguing: What Aristotle, Lincoln and Homer Simpson Can Teach Us about the Art of Persuasion*. New York: Three Rivers.

Herrington, Anne, and Maria Curtis. 2000. *Persons in Process: Four Stories of Writing Development in College*. Urbana, IL: NCTE.

Hersh, Richard H. n.d. "Collegiate Learning Assessment (CLA): Defining Critical Thinking, Analytical Reasoning, Problem Solving and Writing Skills." *Teagle Foundation*. Accessed June 19, 2014. https://hct-portal.hct.ac.ae/support/ctl/IAssessment/introduction/COLLEGIATE_LEARNING_ASSESSMENT.pdf.

Hill, Carolyn Ericksen. 1990. *Writing from the Margins*. New York: Oxford University Press.

Holbrook, Sue Ellen. 1988. "Women's Work: The Feminizing of Composition." Paper presented at the Conference on College Composition and Communication, St. Louis, MO.

hooks, bell. 1990. *Yearning: Race, Gender, and Cultural Politics*. Boston: South End.

Howe, Florence. 1971. "Identity and Expression: A Writing Course for Women." *College English* 32(8): 863–871. http://dx.doi.org/10.2307/375624.

Huot, Brian. 1996. "Toward a New Theory of Writing Assessment." *College Composition and Communication* 47(4): 549–566. http://dx.doi.org/10.2307/358601.

Huot, Brian. 2002. *(Re)Articulating Writing Assessment for Teaching and Learning*. Logan: Utah State University Press.

Imhof, Margarete. 1998. "What Makes a Good Listener? Listening Behavior in Instructional Settings." *International Journal of Listening* 12(1): 81–105. http://dx.doi.org/10.1080/10904018.1998.10499020.

Imhof, Margarete. 2001. "How to Listen More Efficiently: Self-Monitoring Strategies in Listening." *International Journal of Listening* 15(1): 2–19. http://dx.doi.org/10.1080/10904018.2001.10499042.

Jaggar, Alison M. 1989. "Love and Knowledge: Emotion in Feminist Epistemology." In *Women, Knowledge, and Reality: Explorations in Feminist Philosophy*, edited by Garry and Pearsall, 151–176. Boston: Unwin Hyman. 1989. http://dx.doi.org/10.1080/00201748908602185.

Janusik, Laura A. 2002. "Teaching Listening: What Do We Do? What Should We Do?" *International Journal of Listening* 16(1): 5–39. http://dx.doi.org/10.1080/10904018.2002.10499047.

Jarratt, Susan. 1992. "Performing Feminisms, Histories, Rhetorics." Special Issue, *Rhetoric Society Quarterly* 22(1). http://dx.doi.org/10.1080/02773949209390936.

Jarratt, Susan. 2003. "Feminism and Composition: A Case for Conflict." In *Feminism and Composition: A Critical Sourcebook*, edited by Gesa E. Kirsch, Fay Spencer Maor, Lance Massey, Lee Nickoson-Massey, and Mary P. Sheridan-Rabideau, 263–280. Boston: Bedford / St. Martin's.

Jha, Alok. 2011. "We Must Learn to Love Uncertainty and Failure, Say Leading Thinkers." *The Guardian*, January 14. Accessed June 19, 2014. http://www.theguardian.com/science/2011/jan/15/uncertainty-failure-edge-question.

Jones, Richard G., Jr., and Bernadette Marie Calafell. 2012. "Contesting Neoliberalism through Critical Pedagogy, Intersectional Reflexivity, and Personal Narrative: Queer Tales of Academia." *Journal of Homosexuality* 59(7): 957–981. http://dx.doi.org/10.1080/00918369.2012.699835.

Judd, Nancy. 2011. "Can a Dress Made from Trash Change How You See?" *TEDx* video. http://tedxtalks.ted.com/video/TEDxABQ-Nancy-Judd-Can-a-Dress; search%3Atag%3A%22tedxabq%22. Accessed March 26, 2015.

Julian of Norwich. 2001. "From *Revelations of Divine Love* (c.1390s)." In Ritchie and Ronald 2001, 26–28. Pittsburgh: University of Pittsburgh Press.

Jung, Julie. 2005. *Revisionary Rhetoric, Feminist Pedagogy, and Multigenre Texts.* Carbondale: Southern Illinois Press.

Kiley, Kevin. 2013. "Another Liberal Arts Critic." *Insider Higher Ed,* January 30. Accessed June 19, 2014. http://www.insidehighered.com/news/2013/01/30/north-carolina-governor-joins-chorus-republicans-critical-liberal-arts#sthash.NEpjnYw5.dpbs.

Kim, Dae-Joong. 2011. "The Possibility of Differential Space in a Globalized First Year Composition Class." Unpublished MS.

Kopelson, Karen. 2006. "Of Ambiguity and Erasure: The Perils of Performative Pedagogy." In *Relations, Locations, Positions: Composition Theory for Writing Teachers,* edited by Peter Vandenberg, Sue Hum, and Jennifer Clary-Lemon, 563–570. Urbana, IL: NCTE.

Kotter, J. P. 1982. "What Do Effective Managers Really Do?" *Harvard Business Review* 60(6): 156–167.

Kroll, Barry. 2005. "Arguing Differently." *Pedagogy* 5(1): 37–60. http://dx.doi.org/10.1215/15314200-5-1-37.

Lamb, Catherine. 1991. "Beyond Argument in Feminist Composition." *College Composition and Communication* 42(1): 11–24. http://dx.doi.org/10.2307/357535.

Lamm, Nomy. 2001. "It's a Big Fat Revolution." In Ritchie and Ronald 2001, 454–461. Pittsburgh: University of Pittsburgh Press.

Layton, Lyndsey. 2014. "How Bill Gates Pulled off the Swift Common Core Revolution." *Washington Post,* June 7. Accessed June 11, 2014. http://www.washingtonpost.com/politics/how-bill-gates-pulled-off-the-swift-common-core-revolution/2014/06/07/a830e32e-ec34-11e3-9f5c-9075d5508f0a_story.html.

LeCourt, Donna, and Anna Rita Napoleone. 2011. "Teachers with(out) Class: Transgressing Academic Social Space through Working Class Performances." *Pedagogy* 11(1): 81–108. http://dx.doi.org/10.1215/15314200-2010-018.

Lederman, Doug. 2013. "Public University Accountability 2.0." *Inside Higher Ed,* May 6. Accessed June 19, 2014. https://www.insidehighered.com/news/2013/05/06/public-university-accountability-system-expands-ways-report-student-learning.

Locke, Jill. 2007. "Shame and the Future of Feminism." *Hypatia* 22(4): 146–162. http://dx.doi.org/10.1111/j.1527-2001.2007.tb01325.x.

Logan, Shirley Wilson. 1995. *With Pen and Voice: A Critical Anthology of Nineteenth-Century African-American Women.* Carbondale: Southern Illinois University Press.

Logan, Shirley Wilson. 1999. *"We are Coming": The Persuasive Discourse of Nineteenth Century Black Women.* Carbondale: Southern Illinois University Press.

Lonn, Ella. 1924. "Academic Status of Women on University Faculties." *Journal of the American Association of University Women* 17:5–11.

Loraux, Nicole. (Original work published 1984) 1993. *The Children of Athena.* Translated by Caroline Levine. Princeton: Princeton University Press.

Lorde, Audre. 1984. *Sister Outsider*. Freedom, CA: Crossing Press Feminist Series.

Lorenzo, George, and John Ittelson. 2005. "An Overview of Institutional E-portfolios." *Educause Learning Initiative: Advancing Learning through IT Innovation.* Accessed June 19, 2014. https://net.educause.edu/ir/library /pdf/ELI3002.pdf.

Lu, Min-Zhan, and Bruce Horner. 2013. "Translingual Literacy, Language Difference, and Matters of Agency." *College English* 75(6): 582–607.

Lunsford, Andrea. 1995. *Reclaiming Rhetorica: Women in the Rhetorical Tradition.* Pittsburgh: University of Pittsburgh Press.

Lutz, Catherine. 1988. *Unnatural Emotions: Everyday Sentiments on a Micronesian Atoll and Their Challenge to Western Theory.* Chicago: University of Chicago Press.

Lynch, Dennis A., Diana George, and Marilyn M. Cooper. 1997. "Moments of Argument: Agonistic Inquiry and Confrontational Cooperation." *College Composition and Communication* 48(1): 61–85. http://dx.doi.org/10.2307/358771.

Mairs, Nancy. 2001. "Carnal Acts." In Ritchie and Ronald 2001, 392–400. Pittsburgh: University of Pittsburgh Press.

Maitra, Keya. 2013. "The Question of Identity and Agency in Feminism without Borders: A Mindful Response." *Hypatia* 28(2): 360–376. http://dx.doi .org/10.1111/hypa.12017.

Malinowitz, Harriet. 1995. *Textual Orientations: Lesbian and Gay Students and the Making of Discourse Communities.* Portsmouth, NH: Heinemann.

Mangan, Katherine. 2013. "How Gates Shapes State Higher-Education Policy." *Chronicle of Higher Education,* July 14. Accessed June 11, 2014. http://chroni cle.com/article/How-Gates-Shapes-State/140303/.

Marshall, Margaret. 2004. *Response to Reform: Composition and the Professionalization of Teaching.* Carbondale: Southern Illinois University Press.

McWilliam, Erica, and Caroline Hatcher. 2004. "Emotional Literacy as Pedagogical Product." *Continuum (Perth)* 18(2): 179–189. http://dx.doi.org/10.1080 /1030431042000214988.

Micciche, Laura R. 2007. *Doing Emotion: Rhetoric, Writing, Teaching.* Portsmouth, NH: Boynton/Cook.

Miller, Susan. 1991. *Textual Carnivals: The Politics of Composition.* Carbondale: Southern Illinois University Press.

Moon, Gretchen Flesher. 2003. "The Pathos of Pathos: The Treatment of Emotion in Contemporary Composition Textbooks." In *A Way to Move: Rhetorics of Emotion & Composition Studies,* edited by Dale Jacobs and Laura R. Micciche, 33–42. Portsmouth, NH: Boynton/Cook.

Morga, Alicia. 2011. "Emotional Intelligence: The Forgotten Key to Educational Success." *The Huffington Post,* March 3. Accessed May 28, 2013. http://www .huffingtonpost.com/alicia-morga/emotional-intelligence_b_834234.html.

NCTE Task Force on Writing Assessment. 2013. "NCTE Position Statement on Machine Scored Writing." Accessed June 19, 2014. http://www.ncte.org /positions/statements/machine_scoring.

Nelson, Rebecca. 2013. "Q & A: Jewelry Designer Jessica Mindich: Fighting Gun Violence with Bracelets." *Time,* January 29. Accessed June 11, 2014. http:// style.time.com/2013/01/29/jewelry-designer-jessica-mindich-fighting -gun-violence-with-bracelets/.

Ohmann, Richard, ed. 1971. "Women in the Colleges." Special Issue, *College English* 32 (5).

Orner, Mimi, Janet L. Miller, and Elizabeth Ellsworth. 1996. "Excessive Moments and Educational Discourses That Try to Contain Them." *Educational Theory* 46(1): 71–91. http://dx.doi.org/10.1111/j.1741-5446.1996.00071.x.

Perry, Marc, Kelly Field, and Beckie Supiano. 2013. "The Gates Effect." *Chronicle of Higher Education*, July 14. Accessed June 11, 2014. http://chronicle.com /article/The-Gates-Effect/140323/.

Probyn, Elspeth. 2005. *Blush: Faces of Shame*. Minneapolis: University of Minnesota Press.

Quandahl, Ellen. 2003. "A Feeling for Aristotle: Emotion in the Sphere of Ethics." In *A Way to Move: Rhetorics of Emotion and Composition Studies*, edited by Laura Micciche and Dale Jacobs, 11–22. Portsmouth, NH: Boynton/Cook.

Ratcliffe, Krista. 1999. "Rhetorical Listening: A Trope for Interpretive Invention and a 'Code of Cross-Cultural Conduct.'" *College Composition and Communication* 51(2): 195–224. http://dx.doi.org/10.2307/359039.

Ratcliffe, Krista. 2005. *Rhetorical Listening: Identification, Gender, Whiteness*. Carbondale: Southern Illinois University Press.

Rayner, Alice. 1993. "The Audience: Subjectivity, Community, and the Ethics of Listening." *Journal of Dramatic Theory and Criticism* 7(2): 3–24.

Readings, Bill. 1996. *The University in Ruins*. Cambridge, MA: Harvard University Press.

Reese, Susan. 2009. "Are You Listening?" *Techniques: Connecting Education and Careers* 84(2): 10–11.

Rentfrow, Monica. 2009. "Coming Out 'Disabled.'" Unpublished MS.

Reynolds, Nedra. 1993. "Ethos as Location: New Sites for Understanding Discursive Authority." *Rhetoric Review* 11(2): 325–338. http://dx.doi.org/10.1080 /07350199309389009.

Rich, Adrienne. 1979. "Toward a Woman-Centered University." In *On Lies, Secrets, and Silence: Selected Prose*, 125–156. New York: Norton.

Rich, Adrienne. 1986. "Notes toward a Politics of Location." In *Blood, Bread, and Poetry: Selected Prose*, 210–231. New York: Norton.

Ritchie, Joy S., and Kathleen Boardman. 1999. "Feminism in Composition: Inclusion, Metonymy, and Disruption." *College Composition and Communication* 50(4): 585–606. http://dx.doi.org/10.2307/358482.

Ritchie, Joy S., and Kate Ronald, eds. 2001. *Available Means: An Anthology of Women's Rhetoric(s)*. Pittsburgh: University of Pittsburgh Press.

Rowe, Aimee Carrillo. 2005. "Be Longing: Toward a Feminist Politics of Relation." *NWSA Journal* 17(2): 15–46. http://dx.doi.org/10.2979/NWS.2005.17.2.15.

Royster, Jacqueline Jones. 2000. *Traces of a Stream: Literacy and Social Change among African American Women*. Pittsburgh: University of Pittsburgh Press.

Royster, Jacqueline Jones, and Gesa E. Kirsch. 2012. *Feminist Rhetorical Practices: New Horizons for Rhetoric, Composition and Literacy Studies*. Carbondale: Southern Illinois University Press.

Rudd, Calena. 2013. "Internet Censorship." Unpublished MS.

Ryan, Kathleen. 2006. "Recasting Recovery and Gender Critique as Inventive Arts: Constructing Edited Collections in Feminist Rhetorical Studies." *Rhetoric Review* 25(1): 22–40. http://dx.doi.org/10.1207/s15327981rr2501_2.

Sambol-Tosco, Kimberly. 2004. "The Slave Experience: Education, Arts, and Culture," *PBS Educational Broadcasting Corporation.* Accessed June 11, 2014. http://www.pbs.org/wnet/slavery/experience/education/history2.html.

Sandoval, Chela. 2000. *Methodology of the Oppressed.* Minneapolis: University of Minnesota Press.

Sathiyaseelan, Sinduja. 2011. "Negotiating the Bi-nary: Strategic Ambiguity and the Non-nameable Identity in the Classroom." Unpublished MS.

Saunders, Daniel. 2010. "Neoliberal Ideology and Public Higher Education in the United States." *Journal for Critical Education Policy Studies* 8(1): 42–77.

Schell, Eileen E. 1997. *Gypsy Academics and Mother Teachers.* Portsmouth, NH: Heinemann.

Senechal, Diane. 2013. "Measure against Measure: Responsibility versus Accountability in Education." *Arts Education Policy Review* 114(2): 47–53. http://dx .doi.org/10.1080/10632913.2013.769828.

Slaughter, Sheila, and Gary Rhoades. 2004. *Academic Capitalism and the New Economy: Markets, State, and Higher Education.* Baltimore, MD: Johns Hopkins University Press.

Smith, Scott Andrew. 2003. "One the Desk: Dwarfism, Teaching, and the Body." In Freedman and Holmes 2003, 23–34.

Soliday, Mary. 1999. "Class Dismissed." *College English* 61(6): 731–741. http:// dx.doi.org/10.2307/378954.

Spelman, Elizabeth. 1989. "Anger and Insubordination." In *Women, Knowledge, and Reality: Explorations in Feminist Philosophy,* edited by Garry and Pearsall, 263–274. Boston: Unwin Hyman.

Swenson, Jennifer. 2013. "Miscommunication: The Controversy over Bilinguial Education in America." Unpublished MS.

Tannen, Deborah. 1999. *The Argument Culture: Stopping America's War with Words.* New York: Ballantine Books.

Thaiss, Chris, and Terry Myers Zawacki. 2006. *Engaged Writers and Dynamic Disciplines: Research on the Academic Writing Life.* Portsmouth, NH: Boynton/Cook.

Thiem, Annika. 2008. *Unbecoming Subjects: Judith Butler, Moral Philosophy, and Critical Responsibility.* New York: Fordham University Press. http://dx.doi.org /10.5422/fso/9780823228980.001.0001.

Think Progress. 2008. "Media Torn over Whether to Cast Clinton as 'Weak' or 'Calculating' for 'Emotional' Display." *Thinkprogress.org,* January 7. Accessed June 16, 2014. http://thinkprogress.org/media/2008/01/07/18691/clinton -tears/.

Treanor, Paul. "Neoliberalism: Origins, Theory, Definition." Last modified December 2, 2005. http://web.inter.nl.net/users/Paul.Treanor/neoliberalism.html.

Truth, Sojourner. 2001. "Speech at the Woman's Rights Convention, Akron Ohio." In Ritchie and Ronald 2001, 144–145. Pittsburgh: University of Pittsburgh Press.

U.S. News and World Report. 2009. "Obama Slams Wall Street over 'Shameful' Bonuses." *Usnews.com,* January 30. Accessed June 2, 2009.

Valenti, Jessica. 2014. "Hillary Clinton's Book Is Exactly as 'Safe' as Female Politicians Are Forced to Be." *The Guardian,* June 11. Accessed June 17, 2014. http://www.theguardian.com/commentisfree/2014/jun/11/hillary-clinton -book-hard-choices-boring.

Vandenberg, Peter, Sue Hum, and Jennifer Clary-Lemon, eds. 2006. *Relations, Locations, Positions: Composition Theory for Writing Teachers.* Urbana, IL: NCTE.

Villanueva, Victor. 1993. *Bootstraps: From and American Academic of Color.* Urbana, IL: NCTE.

Villanueva, Victor, and Geneva Smitherman. 2003. *Language and Diversity in the Classroom: From Intention to Practice.* Carbondale: Southern Illinois University Press.

Voluntary System of Accountability. 2014. Association of Public and Land Grant Universities. Accessed June 19, 2014. http://www.voluntarysystem.org/.

Warner, Gregory. 2010. "I Understand Your Frustration." *Marketplace.org,* July 6.

Weber, Brenda R. 2010. "Teaching Popular Culture through Gender Studies: Feminist Pedagogy in a Postfeminist and Neoliberal Academy?" *Feminist Teacher* 20(2): 124–138. http://dx.doi.org/10.5406/femteacher.20.2.0124.

Welch, Nancy. 2005. "Living Room: Teaching Public Writing in a Post-publicity Era." *College Composition and Communication* 56(3): 470–492.

White House. 2013. "Fact Sheet on the President's Plan to Make College More Affordable: A Better Bargain for the Middle Class." The White House, Office of Press Secretary. Accessed June 19, 2014. https://www.whitehouse.gov/the-press-office/2013/08/22/fact-sheet-president-s-plan-make-college-more-affordable-better-bargain-.

Williams, Patricia. 2001. "The Death of the Profane." In Ritchie and Ronald 2001, 409–415. Pittsburgh: University of Pittsburgh Press.

Worsham, Lynn. 1998. "Going Postal: Pedagogic Violence and the Schooling of Emotion." *JAC: A Journal of Composition* 18:213–245.

Zawacki, Terry Myers, E. Shelley Reid, Ying Zhou, and Sarah E. Baker. 2009. "Voices at the Table: Balancing the Needs and Wants of Program Stakeholders to Design a Value Added Writing Assessment Plan." *Across the Disciplines* 6. Accessed June 19, 2014. http://wac.colostate.edu/atd/assessment/zawacki etal.cfm.

ABOUT THE AUTHOR

SHARI J. STENBERG is professor of English and composition program director at the University of Nebraska–Lincoln, where she teaches courses in writing, pedagogy, and feminist rhetorics. She is the author of *Professing and Pedagogy: Learning the Teaching of English* and *Composition Studies through a Feminist Lens.* Her essays appear in *College English, College Composition and Communications, Pedagogy,* and *Composition Studies.*

INDEX

Made in the USA
San Bernardino, CA
30 December 2018